BLACK BELT LEADERSHIP 101

WHAT IT TAKES TO BE A BLACK BELT LEADER IN LIFE

With Companion Discussion Guide

John L. Terry, III

ISBN # 9781728966595

Table of Contents

Acknowledgments

All quotations cited in this book are credited to the author. Where possible, the source is provided alongside the quotation. These sources and other valuable leadership resources are included in the Recommended Reading section of this book. Dictionary definitions are cited from Dictionary.com or the Merriam-Webster Dictionary Online.

First edition published, May 2020. ISBN # 9781728966595

This book has been birthed over many hours of research, study and conversation with leadership experts, martial arts school owners and instructors, and a lot of late nights fleshing out this narrative into a cohesive format.

It is my hope that this book will add value to your life, and inspire you to pursue leadership as a lifestyle. Whether you've ever trained in the martial arts or not, you CAN become a Black Belt in Leadership if you will commit to a lifetime of learning and leading.

If you ARE a martial arts instructor (or anyone who works with youth and young adults), I hope you will take on the added role of raising yourself up as a Black Belt Leader in Life so you can mold and shape the students in your school (or organization) to do likewise. Can you imagine a generation of disciplined, respectful, well-mannered black belt students who are also transformational leaders in their local communities?

DEDICATION

To my Mom and Dad, the first leaders and mentors in my life.
Thank you both for leading our family well and starting me on my
own growth journey to become a Black Belt Leader in Life.

To Larry Pyle, for being a mentor and a friend for many years.
Thank you for your tutelage, your wisdom and your willingness to
speak into my life and for challenging me to keep going.

To Professor Marty Cale for the privilege of serving alongside you
for 8 years in one of the premier martial arts associations in the
world, expanding my knowledge of the global martial arts and
entrusting me to lead this organization as your successor.

To John Maxwell, Mark Cole, Paul Martinelli, Christian Simpson,
Roddy Galbraith, Chris Simpson and the global John Maxwell Team
Faculty for pouring into me and inspiring me to develop the leader
within, and to put my dreams to the test.

To Wayne Nance, who taught me how to live Real Life. Thank you
for your wisdom and insight into understanding into the uniqueness
of how our attitudes shape our view of relationships, money, health
and wellness, communication and leadership.

To my wife, Yury, and my children, for allowing me to lead, and
trusting my leadership over the years. I am truly blessed.

To Muffy...Go Change the World!

John L. Terry, III
March 15, 2020

INTRODUCTION

My martial arts journey began in 1973 when my Dad accepted a new position as a salesman that required relocation from Fort Smith AR to the small lakeside community of Russellville. We loaded the U-Haul and made the 70+ mile transition to small town Arkansas.

For me, it was a chance to begin again in a new school, make new friends and experience all the incredible adventures that a small, lakeside town nestled at the base of the Ozark National Forest had to offer.

Being the new kid in a school can be difficult. Being an outsider, not growing up in small-town Arkansas, can be even more difficult. While many of the students were friendly and receptive, I soon found myself the target of others who were "not so nice". Yes, I was bullied.

My Dad soon learned of my troubles at school and he had a solution. He took me downtown and enrolled me in martial arts classes. It was "old school" training...concrete floors, no air conditioning, no pads and no other kids in class. My dad was paying for me to get beat up twice a week, so I could learn to defend myself.

I trained in that school for some time, gaining confidence and learning not only how to defend myself but how to avoid confrontation in the first place. It was a revelation that changed how I lived life. The training instilled in me the belief that anything was possible. I was intrigued by the self-defense aspects of karate and dabbled in other styles to learn variations of these techniques. In time, I became quite skilled as a self-defense practitioner.

Martial arts training was also one of my first introductions into the world of leadership. My instructors not only spent time developing my physical skill set, but they also began to instill me a sense of responsibility that martial artists were to be role models.

I first saw this in class, as we would line up according to rank. White belt students were in the back of the room and black belts were in the front, leading. The various colored belt students filled in the middle. Part of their advancement came not only from their ability to demonstrate proficiency in new techniques but also in their ability to effectively teach and train those who were behind them in rank. It was leadership in action.

As I added color to my belt, with that came not only the responsibility to become proficient at my Art, but to also help our Sensei teach new students in the school. I learned early on that the pursuit of a black belt was also the pursuit of becoming a transformational leader.

In 1993, my Dad introduced me to leadership guru, John Maxwell. An avid reader himself, Dad presented me a copy of John's book, *Developing the Leader Within You*, and following in my dad's footsteps, I read and re-read these powerful truths, and began applying these transformational truths to my life.

Fast forward a few years and my youngest son, Joshua, began to express an interest in the martial arts. He began training with an old schoolmate, Rockie Richardson, who was now teaching in a local dojo in Russellville AR. Shortly thereafter, Jordan opted to join the program, and now two of my boys were punching, kicking and having the time of their lives.

Next thing I knew, I was training alongside both of my boys in yet another martial arts system and we were all competing in a 4-state circuit (and we kept winning). I held forms, weapons and fighting titles for 3 consecutive years and my youngest son also took top honors in his age group for two years.

It was in this dojo we saw the "dark side" of leadership from the Senior Instructor. While an accomplished artist in his given martial art, he was not a man of good morals and did not embrace leadership as a lifestyle. When his photograph, and a video of his arrest, made the statewide news as part of a law enforcement sting, the vast majority of students and instructors refused to train at the school any longer.

The school ultimately closed its door and I found myself being approached by parents from the school to teach their children. I took on a partner and we opened a martial arts school in the waiting room of the financial services firm I owned, with an initial enrollment of four students.

From there, word got out as to what we were doing, and the kids kept coming. We moved to a 1250 square foot downtown storefront, then 2000 square feet, and then settled in a 3000-square foot facility. We acquired a second location in another city, and duplicated success there as well.

What set us apart from the other good schools in the area was our focus on teaching black belt excellence as leaders in life. We expected our students to perform at a high level, both in the dojo and in the classroom (or workplace, if they were adults).

We rewarded academic excellence, encouraged the value of leadership and continually created opportunities for that to be fostered. We watched as our students gave back to their

3

community in some amazing ways. We constantly reminded them that character matters, and as martial artists, they are leaders in life – modeling the virtues of discipline, honor, respect, and self-sacrifice as an example for others to embrace.

It has been exciting to see these students embrace the call to pursue black belt excellence as leaders in life and go on to lead well in their personal and professional lives.

In 2008 I was inducted into the United States Martial Arts Hall of Fame and with that an invitation to join the organization's Board of Directors. I've been privileged to meet and work with world-class instructors from across the globe. It's also broadened the audience to teach and train the value of transformational leadership.

While there are many great martial arts instructors out there teaching amazing techniques, many of these men and women have yet to see and embrace the opportunity before them to not only raise up great martial artists, but also a new generation of transformational leaders who live out the attributes of Black Belt Excellence each and every day of their lives.

But it is not only martial arts instructors who are missing the opportunity to embrace leadership as a lifestyle. There is a leadership deficit in society today, and that has generational ramifications in our homes, churches & synagogues, businesses, classrooms and volunteer organizations.

True transformational leaders can (and should) exhibit these same attributes in their lives as well. Discipline, respect, honor, and self-sacrifice – all are qualities that effective leaders embrace and call their own.

John Maxwell, one of my mentors, says, *"Everything rises and falls on leadership."* I wholeheartedly agree. Where there is a lack of leadership, there is a huge void that stifles creativity and growth. Without effective leadership, society crumbles and ultimately disintegrates.

We need more inspirational, transformational leaders in our world today. Anyone can lead, and in fact, everyone is leading in some way. The real question is how well are you leading – and who is following your lead?

YES...You, too, can lead like a Black Belt!

It's a powerful way to lead, and the making of a black belt leader is within your grasp. Like any other type of training, it's a process that takes time, commitment and dedication. It is something you can do – if you're willing.

To all of you who desire to be true, transformational leaders, this book is written. I hope you will all embrace the challenge and the calling to pursue Black Belt Excellence as Leaders in Life.

So, let's get started on your transformational Black Belt Leadership journey...

Lead Like a Black Belt
Chapter One

Bruce Lee, Chuck Norris, Steven Segal, Jet Li, Jackie Chan, Chow Yun Fat, Wesley Snipes, Donny Yen, Bill Wallace, Michelle Yeoh, Jeff Speakman, Randy Couture, Ronda Rousey, George St. Pierre... household names for those of us who love martial arts.

Many of us grew up watching these amazing individuals display their martial arts prowess on the Big Screen. Who can forget Bruce Lee and Chuck Norris and their immortal deathmatch in the Roman Colosseum? Do you remember Bruce Lee as the amazing Kato in The Green Hornet? How about Jackie Chan and Jet Li in the Chinese cult-classic movie, *"The Forbidden Kingdom"*?

While these talented individuals have impressed us with their incredible displays of martial arts mastery, they all had their humble origins as a white belt beginner under the tutelage of a martial arts instructor. It doesn't matter the system they were taught, they all follow a similar course of study that can be applied to a course in leadership training.

I remember my dad's martial arts journey. Just before his 70th birthday, I found him at home exercising to a Billy Blank's Tae-Bo tape. After teasing him for a few minutes, I reminded him I had a karate school across town and he should come there to train. His response, *"I'm too old for the martial arts."*

For his 70th birthday, I presented my dad a Karate Gi (uniform) along with a certificate for a free month of classes. He donned his uniform and came to class. Five years later, I had the privilege of sitting on his black belt testing panel and watching my dad complete his pursuit of a black belt at the age of 75.

It was the culmination of 5 years of demanding work, diligence and a "don't quit" attitude that helped my dad rise through the ranks and ultimately earn his coveted black belt. *What we are passionate about, we pursue.*

Just like my dad was not too old to pursue black belt excellence, it's never too late (or too early) for you to start on the pursuit of black belt excellence as a leader in life.

Are you passionate about becoming a black belt in leadership?

Are you willing to commit the time, energy and effort to walk through the ranks and earn your coveted black belt in true, transformational leadership?

If so, let's set the stage for what is to come.

Gichin Funakoshi is credited with establishing a colored ranking system to codify martial arts training in ancient Japan. Prior to that, there were only two belt ranks, white and black. In ancient Okinawa, the founders of what is known today as Karate taught their students the essence of their Art. Once a student demonstrated a high degree of competence, along with the loyalty and trust of the Sensei, he was awarded a black belt. This was a sign that he was now a serious student and could be trusted to learn the finer aspects of the teacher's given fighting system.

So, the black belt was not an end – it was the sign of a new beginning. Black belt students were taught at a deeper level, as they had earned the respect of the instructor who was willing to invest additional time and training. This often included weapons training, advanced self-defense instruction as well as how to lead other students in a teaching environment.

Black belt students were also given the responsibility to help teach new students the basics. They would also raise up future serious students who could be recognized by the Master Instructor as worthy of advanced training. They were often referred to as "disciples", visual representations of their Senior Instructor. It was from this inner circle group of "disciples" (serious students) that an inheritor was selected, who would perpetuate the teaching of the Master's system after his demise.

In the pursuit of a black belt in leadership, we too must start with the basics and demonstrate proficiency. Only after we can show competency with the basics that our Master Instructor (Coach or Mentor) can teach us the deeper truths of true, transformational leadership.

Along the way, you will be challenged. There will be times the work becomes tedious, repetitive and monotonous. Such is the way of training. There will be times you want to give up on your journey, to quit. It is in such times that you are truly tested – that your true character is revealed.

There will be times when the process is painful. You can't learn martial arts without some pain and discomfort. Punching, kicking, blocking, parrying, takedowns and joint-locking are not without pain – whether you're on the giving or receiving end. But pain can be a teacher. Pain can prepare us to not panic when we face dangerous situations or circumstances.

In your leadership journey, you too will face times that are painful. You will face challenges, situations, and circumstances that can be dangerous to your future growth and development. It is the maturity of training that can help you make wise choices that will result in a positive outcome that leads you closer to your goal of becoming a black belt leader in life.

There will be times of testing. Each rank advancement has specific techniques that must be demonstrated with proficiency. Your skill set will be evaluated, tweaked and questioned by those above you. If successful, you will earn a new color on your belt, and the privilege to learn additional technique and application of your Art. This is confirmation you're moving down your chosen path – a great motivator to keep the course.

There will be additional responsibilities placed on you as you progress down the path of black belt excellence as a leader in life. At the end of his life on earth, Jesus gave the responsibility to his disciples to *"Go, Teach and Make Disciples."* Each Master Instructor does the same of his students, reminding them as you have been taught, so you are to model so others may learn. To borrow a phrase from Uncle Ben to his young ward, Peter Parker, *"With great power comes great responsibility."*

One of my close friends and martial arts instructors was Sir Richard Bustillo, who passed unexpectedly in 2017. He and Dan Inosanto, both students of Bruce Lee, are credited with bringing about a revival of the martial arts in the Philippines (after WW2 nearly decimated martial arts training on the islands).

Uncle Sifu, as he was lovingly known to my children, was a representative of the Bruce Lee Foundation. Every time Sir Richard would teach, he would remind his audience of his martial arts lineage and the fact they too would represent the life and legacy of Bruce Lee having trained with one of his students. He understood his authority (as a student of one of the greatest martial artists of history) to teach with integrity, and his personal responsibility to represent the organization with dignity, respect, and honor.

You too will be the sum total of the men and women who you've given the opportunity to invest in your life. In exchange for the time, talent, resources and life experience they have chosen to pour into your life also is the responsibility to use that wisely and to live your life in such a way as to pay tribute to their legacy.

That being said, let's look at what a course of black belt leadership looks like. Remember, earning a black belt is not the end. It is merely the beginning of a process by which you earn the right to go deeper and become a true disciple (a serious student) dedicated to a lifetime of learning how to be a transformational leader.

Traditional martial arts break the process of earning a black belt down to a series of levels or steps – each defined by a different colored belt. Our journey toward a black belt in leadership will be no different.

To lead like a black belt, we must gain basic mastery of several key concepts or qualities that every leader should embrace and call their own. To make it easy to understand, we will break it down as follows:

White Belt	Level One	**B**elieve
Yellow Belt	Level Two	**L**earn
Orange Belt	Level Three	**A**ccountability
Green Belt	Level Four	**C**ommunication
Blue Belt	Level Five	**K**inetic
Purple Belt	Level Six	**B**oldness
Brown Belt 1	Level Seven	**E**xcellence
Brown Belt 2	Level Eight	**L**oyalty
Brown Belt 3	Level Nine	**T**ransformation
Black Belt	Level Ten	**LEADERSHIP**

Each of these character traits of effective black belt leadership will be covered in a separate chapter. To get the most out of this course, your focus must be to not just learn the material – but to incorporate into the very fabric of your life. It must become a part of who you are.

You should read this book through in its entirety to get a general understanding of each of the core leadership attributes on your journey to black belt excellence as a leader in life. That's the starting point for effective learning and personal development.

You should then set aside the next 9 months to focus on internalizing each of these character attributes in your life, so they become an integral part of who you are. That builds discipline and consistency in your personal growth journey toward becoming a black belt leader.

You should spend 30 days on each quality of leadership, practicing it until it becomes a part of your daily routine. For example, Chapter Two focuses on your belief in yourself – that you can become a black belt in transformational leadership. For the next 30 days that should become your focus. You then move on to Chapter Three and add that attribute, while still practicing what you learned from Chapter Two.

At the end of 9 months, you will have internalized nine distinct leadership attributes into your life and demonstrated that you're now ready to become a serious student of true, transformational leadership. You will walk with a new sense of confidence and will discover new opportunities to lead yourself and others.

To help you on your leadership journey, you'll find a companion Discussion Guide at the end of this book. Whether you're reading this book alone, as part of a mastermind or small group study, or you're discussing this in a classroom setting, this guide will prompt you to reflect on what you've read. Think through the application of each of these attributes, and implement a plan to become a Black Belt Leader In Life.

No one takes their martial arts journey alone. After all, you can't practice punching, kicking, blocking, throwing, joint locking, and joint manipulation without a partner. It takes teamwork to accomplish greatness – in any endeavor. As one of my mentors, John Maxwell, says, *"One is too small a number to achieve greatness."* (The Law of Significance)

King Solomon of Ancient Israel wrote that *"two are better than one, for they have a good reward for their labor."* We'll spend more time on this topic in Chapter Four (Accountability), but for now, let me say there is immense value in going through this study with another person (or a small group of people) as part of a mastermind group. There is great value in learning together.

By the way, there are typically 10 degrees (levels) of black belt in most martial arts disciplines. Earning your 1st-degree black belt isn't the end – it's the start of the next chapter of personal development in your life. The same can be said of leadership.

It's a lifelong quest to be more effective at leading yourself and others. It's a lifetime commitment to learning, modeling and living out the qualities and attributes of true, transformational leadership.

So, let's don your Gi, cinch up your belt, line up on the floor and get ready to start your training.

The Power of Believing
Chapter Two

"As a man thinketh in his heart, so is he." These are among the wise sayings of King Solomon. In the early 1900s, James Allen reminded us in his classic work, *"As a Man Thinketh"* that we can't become without believing.

Dr. Dan Netherland held several world records for strength and demonstrations of power breaking. His son, Chad, has appeared on Stan Lee's *"Superhuman"* TV series. Their feats of skill include breaking 2000 pounds of concrete and ice respectively. They are truly super-human individuals who can perform amazing feats of strength, dazzling audiences around the world.

One of the keys to their success is a belief in themselves that they can do the *"impossible"*. Dr. Dan, Chad, and any martial arts professional who performs at a world-class level (like that of any professional athlete) all start with an undoubting belief in themselves.

In 1954, Roger Bannister, a medical student, became the first human to break the 4-minute mile. For years, scientists had studied the human anatomy, physics, and acceleration only to determine that man was incapable of breaking the 4-minute mile. It was an anatomical and medical impossibility.

But Roger Bannister believed in himself, and his ability to do what no other human had done before him. On May 6, 1954, at the Iffley Road Track in Oxford, England, Roger Bannister recorded a time of 3:59.4 minutes. He shattered traditional belief of what mankind can do, and today breaking the 4-minute mile has become the standard for world-class athletes in this race.

In 2008 I was inducted into the United States Martial Arts Hall of Fame for my advocacy work in teaching anti-bully, predator awareness, and rape & assault prevention programs in schools and universities in the U.S. In my "Women-Safe" program, we often use board breaking as a mental motivator to convince women they are stronger than they think.

> *"As a man (or woman) thinks, so he (or she) becomes."*
>
> King Solomon

It's exciting to watch a woman taking the class step up to break her first board. After walking through the mechanics, we spend a few minutes in the class talking them through the value of believing in themselves. Then, the candidate winds up and amazes herself (and the rest of the class) when she shatters the board in two.

"As a man (or woman) thinks, so he (or she) becomes..."

The Power of Belief is the starting point for becoming a leader. Why? **You cannot become what you do not believe.** It's a core dynamic in learning to become a black belt in leadership. If you cannot see yourself as a leader, there is no sense starting the journey. So, let's start with three essential, gut-check questions:

(Q) Do you see yourself as leadership material?

(Q) Do you believe that you have what it takes to be an effective leader?

(Q) Are you willing to believe in yourself to do what is necessary to become a black belt in leadership?

If you answered YES to these three questions, then congratulations. You've taken your first rank assessment toward earning a black belt in effective leadership.

I believe there are FOUR key beliefs that you must embrace to be effective as a leader in life. Let's examine each of these core beliefs and understand their role in your personal leadership development.

1. Believe in the Value of Leadership

There is value in leadership. If you don't believe that, there is no sense moving forward with this study. In his classic book, *"Developing The Leader Within You"*, leadership guru John Maxwell says, *"The effectiveness of your work will never rise above your ability to lead and influence others. You cannot produce consistently on a level higher than your leadership."*

Without leadership, there would be no great discoveries on earth. Columbus would not have discovered America. Armstrong would not have walked on the Moon. Henry Ford would not have invented the Model T. Every discovery we have seen in the earth has come from an individual who believed in the value of leadership, because leaders are innovators, creators, explorers, and change agents.

In the animal kingdom, the lion is considered the King of the Beasts. Around the world, the lion is used to symbolize leadership, power, and strength. Alexander the Great's father, Phillip of Macedonia, said, *"An army of deer led by a lion is more to be feared than an army of lions led by a deer."* Author Mark Sanborn added, *"An army of lions led by a lion is to be feared most of all, for it is unstoppable."*

In his book, *"You Don't Need a Title to be a Leader"*, Mark Sanborn also notes, *"People who lead – whether or not they have a title – strive to make things better."* That's the true value of leadership.

The Okinawan islands were plagued by pirates and thieves at the end of the 19th century. Anko Itosu, a tiny man of unassuming stature, is credited with codifying a system of self-defense that ultimately became known as Karate. Itosu sought to make things better on his island nation by training others to defend themselves and ultimately gave birth to one of the most practiced martial arts systems in the world. Itosu demonstrated the value of leadership – as true leaders make the world a better place by their actions. (More on Anko Itosu in the chapters to come.)

Ronald Reagan understood the value of leadership as he took on the Soviet Union. His willingness to call for an end of the division of Europe into East and West became a clarion call for others to follow – eventually leading to the historic images of the Berlin Wall coming down and seeing the once-divided city united again.

Tom Brady understands the value of leadership. One of the greatest quarterbacks to play the game, Brady takes his role as a leader seriously, as he understands there can be no victory without effective leadership. To watch him lead his team to win after win, despite overwhelming odds at times, demonstrates the value of leadership when it comes to winning – which is something leaders do well.

I've heard my mentor, John Maxwell, say numerous times, *"Leadership is influence."* The value of leadership is the ability to influence the lives of others and to bring about positive life-change, adding value in the process. Without leadership, there is no influence. Without influence, people will never achieve their full potential.

2. Believe in the Need for Leadership

Not only must a leader believe in the value of leadership. A leader must also believe there is a NEED for leadership. A leader sees a cause or a calling before others do, and rallies others to embrace it as their own.

Mahatma Gandhi, Nelson Mandela, Martin Luther King Jr., and Mother Teresa are all examples of leaders who embraced a cause (or a calling) and rallied others to come alongside to bring about positive life-change in the lives of a nation as a result. The movie "Braveheart" documents the life and legacy of William Wallace, a fearless leader who understood the need for leadership to secure freedom and independence for the Scottish people.

The need for leadership can be seen in today's fractured marriages and families. It can be seen in the deficit of leadership in churches and synagogues in America and other parts of the world. The need for leadership can be seen in the corruption in politics and business. We need leaders who are willing, and able, to effectively lead in virtually every segment of society today.

One of the greatest inventors in America's history was Thomas Edison. Among his revolutionary inventions are the light bulb, the phonograph, the mimeograph, the movie camera, electric power distribution, and the world's first industrial research library. Edison led a crack team of inventors who were all focused on improving the quality of life for all Americans, and exporting that technology to the rest of the civilized world.

Edison understood the need for leadership. Without the ability to assemble and lead a team of like-minded individuals, the innovations that have made modern living possible might never have been invented. Together, they embarked on a mission to accomplish what at the time seemed impossible. Today that same spirit of innovation and creativity inspires a new generation of scientists to tackle some of humanity's greatest challenges.

3. Believe in Your Calling to be a Leader

Not only do you have to believe in the value of leadership, and the need for leadership, you must believe that you have been called to lead. This is the quintessential belief you must start with if you intend to pursue black belt excellence as a leader in life.

As I said earlier, you cannot become what you do not believe. In my many years as a martial arts instructor, trainer and coach, I've watched many people sign up for classes, unsure of their talent or ability. From the onset, our instructors sought to establish an *"I can"* mindset in the students. Because if they don't believe it, they can't achieve it. By the same token, if they can believe it, nothing is impossible to them.

The same is true of anyone who wants to lead in some area. Belief in yourself is essential if you want to see success in any endeavor you pursue. Understand this...If you don't believe you CAN do "it" (whatever "it" may be), you have chosen to believe you CAN'T do "it" by default. Remember, *"As a man (or woman) thinks, so he (or she) becomes..."*

You must believe you have been called to lead, to influence the lives of others, to be an agent for change in the world around you. That's the calling of leadership.

Bill Clinton believed in his calling as a leader. Born in the small town of Hope, AR, he and his mother relocated to Hot Springs AR during his school years. One of my long-time friends, Doug Harris, shared a personal story from his childhood that speaks to believing in your calling.

Doug recounted his being in class with Bill Clinton while in Junior High. Each person was asked to stand and tell the class what their vocational plans were, post-graduation. While most of the students shared their plans for college or career choices, Doug remembered that when Bill Clinton was called upon to give his answer, he stood and told his classmates, "*I will be President of the United States.*" Even at an early age, Mr. Clinton was confident in his calling as a leader, and he pursued that calling with a passion which culminated with his becoming the 42nd President of the United States.

I was privileged to meet Sir Edmund Hillary's son a few years ago. He was planning to retrace his father's steps as he became the first man to summit Mt. Everest. Hillary believed in his calling as a leader, and his life was living proof of what he believed.

You must believe in your calling as a leader.

4. Believe You CAN Grow and Mature as a Leader

When I began my training in martial arts, it became evident very quickly that I had a lot to learn. There was always another punch, kick, block, parry or a new stance to learn, practice, and master. Then it was taking those individual movements and putting them into defensive and offensive combinations. Decades later, there is still much left to learn. It is truly a lifetime of learning...and you'll never learn it all.

The same can be said of any professional sport, business endeavor or hobby you want to pursue. I recently spent some time with former members of the Dallas Cowboys football team, many of whom were on one or more Super bowl teams. As we talked about training, a constant among all these talented athletes was the fact that there was always something "new" to learn, something "old" to review (so the skill wasn't lost), and something "more" that could be added to the playbook.

I've been associated with the United States Martial Arts Hall of Fame since 2008, and now serve as this prestigious organization's president. As such, I've had the distinct honor to meet and train with many living legends in the martial arts. One of the things that impressed me about these talented individuals is the fact they are committed to a lifetime of learning when it comes to not only their Art but the martial arts as a whole.

To attend our National Training Camp is an opportunity to train with world-class instructors, representing a broad cross-section of the martial arts. Yet, you will find these very same instructors on the floor when they aren't teaching. They are openly seeking to learn from their fellow instructors, regardless of rank. Even the highly-ranked grandmasters that serve on our Grandmaster's Council are found on the training floor learning from each other, even from those they outrank.

There is ALWAYS something more to learn if you are committed to a lifetime of learning.

My Papaw Newton was a coal miner. After he retired, his pride and joy was his garden, something that he worked at diligently each year. He would take me as a young boy into the garden to learn about corn, beans, peas, carrots, potatoes and other vegetables he would grow. He would always remind me of was the fact that a plant was only good if it was growing. A plant can't produce if it's been uprooted. The roots have to remain firmly planted in the ground.

The same can be said for our need to grow and mature as leaders in life. If we are not constantly investing in our own personal growth as leaders, we have uprooted ourselves from any opportunity to produce fruit in our own lives, or in the lives of others.

Growing and maturing as a leader is invaluable, as you're only effective as a leader when you're growing. In his book, *Leadership 101*, John Maxwell says, *"Personal success without leadership ability brings only limited effectiveness."* You can lead others only to the level of your own leadership ability and if you're not growing you're capping your ability to lead.

Leadership ability, as John Maxwell pointed out, is essential to personal success. Everyone has leadership ability, but the question is to what level are you willing to develop this ability. What sacrifices are you willing to make to hone this ability to truly become a world-class leader in life?

It is said that 10,000 hours of practice is required to become an expert in any given field. If you commit a mere 2 hours a day to practice, that's 5,000 days (13.7 years) to achieve expert status. How many people are willing to truly commit that level of effort to achieve that level of expertise in any area of their lives?

A few years ago, I was invited to represent the United States Martial Arts Hall of Fame at the Pitons Open, an international martial arts competition held at the Olympic Training Center on the island of St. Lucia in the Caribbean. While my breath was taken at the absolute beauty of this island, I was in awe at the level of skill of the competitors who competed in this high-level competition.

One of the most beautiful parts of any martial arts competition (at least to me) is watching kata (forms). A kata is a stylized, sequential group of movements (blocks, punches, kicks, etc.) performed in a pattern. In practice, it was intended to teach "predictable response training" (muscle memory) to students, so they could learn to respond to various attack scenarios instinctively.

In performance, kata is almost a dance. It is a display of strength, power, suppleness, and focus that is beautiful to watch – especially among those who perform this at a high level. In St. Lucia, kata was performed solo, but also in a group setting as synchronized movements.

As these young competitors marched onto the floor, a hush fell across the gymnasium. You could have heard a whisper from the audience. Each team of 3 to 5 would silently assume their positions on the floor, and then with a single command from the leader of the team, they would explode into action.

Like a single unit, each competitor snapped out crisp, concise blocks, kicks, and punches as one. As they moved across the floor, in perfect synchronization, it was as if they were all of one mind. These gifted athletes had taken their natural ability to a level of skill that few in the martial arts world will ever achieve. When each team finished their performance, the audience would erupt in bodacious cheer and applause.

What I learned from talking with their instructors was that these young competitors had been training as a unit since they were small children. They trained 2 to 3 hours a day, 4 to

5 days a week, for 6-8 years or more to get to this intense level of performance. They were not only amazing individual performers, but they were also a unit that thought and moved as one mind.

This was one of the most difficult competitions I've ever had to judge, as the level of competition was among the highest I had experienced to that point. I walked away with an even greater appreciation, and a reminder, that you can achieve the impossible – if you only believe.

Believing you can grow and mature as a leader is no different. We all have a natural ability to lead, and we are all leading in some way. The level to which we cultivate and train this natural ability will determine both the level at which we will perform as a leader and our effectiveness at leading ourselves and others.

SUMMARY – Level One (White Belt)

"Nothing can be achieved that you do not believe."
John Terry

1. Believe in the value of leadership.
2. Believe in the need for leadership.
3. Believe in your calling as a leader.
4. Believe you can grow and mature as a leader.

The Necessity of Learning
Chapter Three

Mahatma Gandhi said, *"Live as if you were to die tomorrow. Learn as if you were to live forever."* From birth, each of us started on a learning journey. Sitting, crawling, walking, talking, feeding, dressing, bathing and grooming ourselves, learning to ride a bicycle, or drive a car is but a minuscule snapshot at all the amazing things we each have had to learn in our lives up to this point in time.

Most of us entered school around the age of 5 or 6. For the next 12 years, we learned to read and write. We learned the basics of science, history, geography, language, art, music and mathematics. Some of us went further, pursuing an advanced degree from a college or university. Others went to a trade school to hone our knowledge and skills of a craft, such as welding, architecture, plumbing, carpentry or electrical wiring.

All along the way, we are also learning how to interact and relate with others. We learn how we communicate and connect with others, as well as what types and styles of communication are required in various business, personal or professional settings.

Relationships are complex, both from a personal and a professional perspective. The idiosyncrasies of how we interact and relate to others are a learning experience that continues throughout our natural lives. Each person we encounter, connect with or partner with in a personal or professional setting requires that we learn how to co-exist, else the relationship is short-lived.

We also spend our lives (hopefully) learning economics, the wise use of money. We must learn how to manage money (budgeting), as well as understand how money works. Insurance, investments, banking, lending, and credit are all learning opportunities as well.

Our life is really a learning university whether we realize this or not. Learning takes place (or should) just about every single day of our lives. No doubt, you've thought of other ways you have been learning and growing personally, as well as professionally, throughout your life.

Should our learning as leaders be any different?   In John Maxwell's book, *The 21 Irrefutable Laws of Leadership,* he discusses the Law of the Lid.   The Law of the Lid essentially says that we can lead only to the level of our ability. Our ability (or inability) to lead puts a lid (a cap or a limit) on our ability to lead ourselves and others.

It is only through our willingness to become lifetime learners of leadership that we can raise our level of influence as leaders and be more effective at leading ourselves and others. That's the **necessity of learning**.

You can't walk into a dojo and expect to walk out as a black belt in one day any more than you can pick up a basketball or football for the first time and expect to be recruited by an NBA or NFL team the same day.   There is a learning process required.

The same can be said of leadership. You can't read a single book, or attend a 2-hour motivational course and immediately be a thought leader in the world of leadership and influence.

I believe there are four key concepts you must embrace if you intend to pursue Black Belt Excellence as a Leader in Life. Let's look at these critical learning facts.

1. Commit to a Lifestyle of Learning

The necessity of learning dictates that learning cannot be a *"one and done"* experience. As discussed in Chapter Two, any topic or skill requires 10,000 hours of practice to become an expert. To go beyond being an expert to become truly world-class, that number could be 50,000 hours or more.

Wayne Nance, the founder of Real Life Management, has spent over 30 years understanding the brain and how it influences the way people think, speak, interact with others and make life choices. As such, he is considered an expert in understanding an individual's mental hard-wiring and soft-wiring, as well as the impact of emotions in the decision-making process. Wayne's organization helps people understand how their decisions around relationships, money, food, fitness, and leadership are shaped and influenced by their mental "attitude". He's truly become a black belt expert in attitudinal leadership.

One of the greatest martial arts legends of recent history is the legendary Bruce Lee. Bruce's life was characterized by a lifetime of learning. His pursuit to learn more about the diverse universe of martial arts allowed Lee to continually adapt and add to his wealth of knowledge of martial arts applications in self-defense and in film. His art (Jeet-Kune-Do) is an eclectic blend of martial arts styles and systems into a "style with no style" that continues to evolve as practitioners use this adaptive fighting system.

Grandmaster Austin Box is a Native American martial arts instructor who has dedicated over 50 years of his life to the martial arts. A veteran of the Vietnam War, Grandmaster Box is a kind, quiet man who has a passion for helping others learn to protect themselves, and to pass on the legacy of what he has learned over the past 50 years to others. Even though in his 80s, he continues to expand his knowledge of the martial arts, seeking to learn what can be added to his wealth of experience to pass on to the next generation of martial arts instructors.

As leaders, we too must commit to a lifetime of learning. Going back to the Law of the Lid, John Maxwell reminds us that our ability limits (caps) our ability to lead. The only way to expand the ability to be a more effective leader is to commit to learning. At a recent John Maxwell conference, John reminded those of us in the room of a quote from Ray Kroc, *"When you're green, you're growing. When you're ripe, you'll start to rot."*

It's a lesson I learned from my Papaw Newton. To continue to grow, you must remain green – keeping your roots firmly planted into the fertile fields of learning. **You'll never achieve a level of expertise that is transformational without committing to a lifetime of learning.**

Brian Tracy said that learning is the minimal obligation for success in any given field. On BrianTracy.com, he blogged, *"Your ability to expand your mind and strive for lifelong learning is critical to your success. By dedicating yourself to learning, you can get ahead in every aspect of your life. All it takes is a commitment."*

A lifetime commitment to learning includes reading. The top leadership professionals read 2-3 hours a day. They attend regular workshops, they spend time with other leaders, and they hire a coach or mentor. They do what is necessary to keep their roots planted deeply in the fertile soil of learning, so they can keep growing and maturing.

It also means listening to podcasts and watching training videos from other leadership professionals. Learning also involves joining professional organizations where ideas can be shared, and ongoing personal and professional development can take place. That's being committed to a lifetime of learning.

2. Leaders Must Grow to be Effective

You don't join a martial arts school to train with a White Belt. You sign up in a martial arts program to train with a black belt because you want to learn from someone who has experience and expertise. You want to train with a seasoned professional who has proven himself or herself as an expert in their field.

Can you imagine learning to cook from someone who has never boiled a pot of water or learning to ride a horse from a person whose only experience riding is the 25-cent ride in front of the grocery store?

How many famous people (celebrities, politicians, or world leaders) would be comfortable traveling with a security team comprised of individuals who had never trained as part of a personal protection detail? Why is the President of the United States protected by an elite group of highly trained Secret Service professionals?

If given the choice, I believe we all prefer to work with people who possess knowledge and experience of the subject matter we are seeking to learn. We all believe we can learn more from working with a proven expert in a given field of study than from a novice with little or no knowledge or experience.

Growth is essential to opportunity. Can you see a toddler of 2 years of age working at the drive-through window of a local

McDonalds? What about a 4-year old driving a taxi or picking you up when you use your Smartphone to summon an Uber driver?

We had to be a certain age to start attending school, to learn how to drive, to get hired for our first real job, open a bank account, sign a legally binding contract or get married. All the time, we were growing physically, mentally and emotionally. With growth comes some level of maturity, along with proven life experience.

First-century church planter, Paul the Apostle, said that those who teach are held to a higher standard than those who don't. Leaders ARE teachers. John Maxwell reminds us that *"A leader is one who knows the way, shows the way and goes the way."* Unless you are learning and growing, you will come to a point that you can lead no further, and you've essentially placed a limit on your ability to effectively lead others.

In ancient Sparta, male children were taken at an early age to begin training as a warrior. From their childhood, they were pushed physically, mentally and emotionally to become elite members of one of the premier fighting forces of ancient history. They were, by today's standards, abused and sometimes mutilated, all in an effort to teach these children to ignore pain and fear and continue fighting. They were taught to wield a variety of weapons, including sword and spear, as well as the proper use of a shield both as an offensive and defensive weapon.

The end result was a fighting force that, according to ancient history, withstood a Babylonian army (vastly superior in number) for three days during the historic Battle of Thermopylae. This epic battle is still studied by military historians and future military leaders.

The Spartans were committed to growing as leaders. They understood their ability to withstand those who would come against their city-state could only be successful if they committed to a lifetime of growing, training, learning and adapting to an ever-changing social/political environment.

As a leader, you must be committed to growing. You may not be called on to stand in the gap to protect your family or your city from invaders, but you WILL be called on to know the way, show the way and go the way.

Every leader needs to be connected to other leaders. It's a growth success strategy. As iron sharpens iron, so do leaders sharpen leaders. The elite leadership thought leaders of recent history have an inner circle of individuals who not only have permission to speak into their lives but to also hold them accountable to remain pliable, flexible and teachable. That's where continued growth can (and will) take place.

You're only effective as a leader if you're growing. You're only growing if you're green. You're green only if you remain connected to the vine, and your roots are firmly planted deep within the fertile soil of learning.

Once you quit learning, you start to rot. And no one wants to follow a rotten leader.

3. Learning Requires Humility and Openness

To commit to becoming a lifetime learner is to admit that you don't know everything. Now let's be honest. For some, this can be hard. If you are prideful or deal with a huge ego, it can be even more so. But humility is required if we are to truly be open to learning and growing to become a world-class, transformational black belt leader in life.

More on Anko Itosu. He was born in 1831 in Shuri, Okinawa. A modest man of small stature, Itosu was an unassuming man who by the end of his life was perhaps one of the most feared men on the island. Referred to by many as the founder of modern karate, he is credited with teaching many of the instructors who in turn spread karate through the island nation, as well as influenced its spread to other nations.

Itosu was accosted by a group of thugs as he traveled between cities on the island. To these bandits, he was easy prey. Yet Itosu is credited with single-handedly disabling his assailants, killing some and wounding the rest. The fame of his encounter led many people on the island to seek his martial arts instruction.

This is where Itosu's humility was displayed. When asked by his students to teach them the best way to deal with multiple assailants, as he had been, his response was classic Itosu, *"When confronted by multiple attackers, your best defense is to run away."* While he could have gloated about his victory and allowed his ego to dictate how he taught, Itosu cared more for the welfare of his students than his ego. He preferred to teach them to avoid confrontation rather than fight.

While Itosu was a gifted teacher and master instructor, he continued to train with his own teacher, acknowledging there was always something more to learn. He remained open to adding to his knowledge base and encouraged his students to do likewise.

Steve Jobs is known as one of the most prolific innovators of recent history. The founder of Apple, Jobs was a talented designer and started a company whose focus remains on challenging the status quo and being a technology innovator.

Yet for all his creative genius, Jobs was forced out of the very company he built.

Jobs could have been bitter, but he chose to be better. He remained open to learning and used his inspiring vision to launch another successful company, NeXT, that was eventually acquired by Apple, and brought Steve Jobs back into leading the Apple brand until his death. His "Think Different" campaign is credited with bringing Apple back from the financial brink to become one of the major technology brands of the early 21st century.

Mark Cole, another of my mentors, worked the phone room of The John Maxwell Company. His job was to "smile and dial" and fill rooms for John Maxwell's upcoming events. It was an entry-level position in the organization, but one that Mark opted to pursue with humility and passion.

Mark shared the story of a chance event that forever changed his life. John Maxwell was scheduled to speak at a function and the person who normally ran his product table at these events was unable to travel. At the last minute, Mark was asked to make the trip to man the table. John Maxwell at this point did not even know Mark Cole's name. It was Mark's opportunity to lead.

On the return trip, John Maxwell asked Mark Cole what the sales statistics were from the event table. Knowing John was a stickler for numbers, Mark made sure he knew how much product had been sold, the ratio of sales to attendees and other important statistics. Mark was able to share the numbers with John, and demonstrate that he could do the job efficiently and effectively.

Mark chuckled when he said, *"After I gave John the numbers, he asked me a second time. When I confirmed our sales were above average, he asked, 'What's your name again?'"* Mark had demonstrated humility and an openness to learn how to do something new – and to help lead in another key area within the Maxwell organization.

Today, Mark Cole is the CEO of John Maxwell's companies and remains one of the humblest men I know. Always looking to add value to the lives of others, Mark is passionate about leadership and equipping others to influence those around them in a positive way. Mark remains open to learning. In fact, he is always learning, growing and maturing as a leadership thought leader.

Even though Mark is a competitive guy, he has chosen to put his ego and pride on the shelf. True leaders are servant leaders who put others before themselves and models this to everyone on the team.

Humility is defined as a modest view of one's importance. Leadership is about modeling a lifestyle before others that inspires them to act in a similar fashion. **Leadership is ACTION!**

> Leadership is action. It's about equipping others with tools, skills and resources, so they can in turn effectively lead others.

It is about equipping others with tools, skills, and resources so they, in turn, can effectively lead others.

Without humility, leaders tend to focus on themselves. At this point, leadership can morph into dictatorship. **Leadership is others-centered.** History is rife with leaders like Benito Mussolini, Adolph Hitler, Joseph Stalin, and Saddam Hussein all who used their power and authority for self-serving purposes.

Without openness, there is no willingness to learn. A mind that is closed to innovative ideas, new ways of learning or new adaptations to current knowledge is a mind that cannot expand. The world around us is always growing, changing and adapting. If you are not open to learning how to adapt to this ever-changing world in which we live, your ability to lead others will be limited.

4. Leaders Must Also Be Followers

One of the most important things I've learned from my years in the martial arts, and as a leader, is that leaders are also followers. As I began my quest for my first black belt, I worked diligently to be the best I could be at each rank along my journey. This earned me the respect of my senior instructors, which in turn opened the door for me to have the privilege to train with other highly ranked Grandmasters in various disciplines of martial arts.

Anko Itosu was a follower of the legendary Sokun Matsumura. Gichin Funakoshi, who formalized karate teachings when he took the art to Japan, was a student of Itosu. Grandmaster Richard Bustillo, one of my mentors and instructors, was a student of Bruce Lee. Each of these talented instructors knew that to be an effective leader and teacher, you must also be a follower.

The concept of discipleship has been with us throughout recorded history. Placing yourself under the tutelage of an experienced teacher is an essential element for achieving extraordinary results. Professional athletes at the highest levels of their game all have a coach or a mentor – someone who can constantly fine-tune their talent, so they can continue to perform at a world-class level. Even celebrities turn to coaches and mentors who can help them hone their craft and stay at the top of their field, be it acting, singing, speaking or dancing.

Who you follow may change as you go through various levels of your personal growth process. Remember the Law of the Lid? There may be times in your development as a leader that you will outgrow the ability of your coach or mentor to lead you any further. When that occurs, it is time to find a new leader to follow who can take you to the next level of your personal development.

Professional athletes, speakers, trainers, and coaches will learn all they can from their coaches and mentors, sometimes spending their entire career with the same guide. There may be situations or circumstances when a change is required. When that occurs, be open to change, as it may be that fresh set of eyes, or a new voice of experience speaking into your life that can make the difference between staying at the same level or going to the next plateau in your personal development.

In the first century A.D., Jesus of Nazareth took 12 men under his discipleship, and these 12 men went on to change the world. Today, over 2.2 billion people worldwide continue to follow the teachings of this individual. The power of discipleship cannot be ignored or minimized in its significance to bring about transformational change.

Leaders are learners. They are committed to a lifetime of learning to continually grow and mature. There is NO arrival for a leader; it is a perpetual journey that will continue as long as there is life on the earth. A leader's role is to prepare those who will continue to journey by leading the next generation once he or she has passed the torch and left this earth.

SUMMARY – Level Two (Yellow Belt)

"A lifetime of learning equips for a lifetime of leading."
John Terry

1. Commit to a lifestyle of learning.
2. Leaders must grow to become effective.
3. Learning requires humility and openness.
4. Leaders must be followers.

The Importance of Accountability
Chapter Four

King Solomon is known for his authorship of Proverbs, also known as *The Book of Wise Sayings*. He is often quoted for his words of wisdom, and his writings are required reading for many who want to succeed in business and in life. Yet for all his words of wisdom, King Solomon failed to follow his own advice.

For all of King Solomon's insights, he failed to be accountable to the very laws that governed his kingdom. He failed to be accountable to the legacy established by his father, King David. As a result, his kingdom was ultimately divided after his demise. What was once a kingdom united became a fractured country that was unable to defend itself from its warring neighbor states was overrun by its foes and its inhabitants were taken into captivity.

In being accountable to no one, King Solomon found himself without a moral compass to guide him, and no one to speak into his life nor challenge and question his poor decision-making. This ultimately led to his failure to effectively lead and influence his generation. Steven Covey said it well when he said, *"Accountability is Response-Ability."*

Actor Stephen Baldwin, having gone through a very difficult season in life, stated, *"I learned in an extremely hard way that the accountability falls with me."* I believe if we are honest, we can all relate to this statement. A lack of accountability often manifests itself in lifestyle choices that are not in our best interest. It is in those moments we wish we had an accountability partner to help us make wise, responsible choices.

As children, we are initially accountable to our parents. Our parents have a legal (and a moral) obligation to raise us, and should we make a mistake, our parents were held responsible. They set our curfew and established the boundaries that governed how we lived our lives.

Over time, we aged and began to take on more personal responsibility. The role of our parents' changed, and we had to assume a greater role in our own decision-making process. The need for each of us to have others who can (and will) speak into our lives and help hold us accountable for our actions, becomes more important.

In the prior chapter, we discussed the fact that world-class athletes and celebrities all utilized coaches, mentors and trainers to keep them in peak performance condition. These coaches often will also serve the role of an accountability partner, helping their clients make wise choices and holding them accountable when they don't.

In the past few years, we've seen that college sports coaches must, at times, step in to hold their student-athletes accountable for poor choices. This can result in disciplinary actions, suspensions or even removal from the team. We've seen similar problems in the professional sports world, corporate America and even in our government. Where there is a lack of accountability, everyone seeks to serve their own interests, all at the expense of others.

ACCOUNTABILITY is an obligation or willingness to accept responsibility or to account for one's actions. A friend who is a Marine says they expand this definition to include the personal obligation that with each Marine's action is an expectation to be personally accountable for that action (or lack thereof).

In martial arts training, mutual accountability is a given. Each student is personally responsible for his or her own advancement. While the instructor is there to guide, teach and critique, it is up to the individual student to apply what they have learned, internalize it and to demonstrate this with proficiency before their instructors during rank advancement testing, as well as in class. When you are standing before a black belt testing panel, the only one accountable for your performance is you.

In life, we all have need of mutual accountability. *"As iron sharpens iron, so are the wounds of a friend,"* according to King Solomon. Being mutually responsible is an essential element to growing and maturing as a leader. Without accountability, your ability to rise to the level of being a transformational leader is limited.

> "I learned in an extremely hard way that the accountability falls with me."
>
> Stephen Baldwin
> *BrainyQuotes.com*

Who do you answer to in life? Who are the people above you, beside you and around you that have your permission to speak into your life, offer words of counsel and have the authority to question your decisions and challenge your choices? If that answer is *"No One"* then you have an accountability deficit in your life.

There are four areas where accountability is key:

1. You Must Be Accountable to Yourself

The first person you must be accountable to is yourself. This is a lesson I learned early in life and something I have taught my children from the time they were very young. It is a life lesson that every leader should learn. Here's my accountability life lesson to my kids:

"Life is a series of choices and consequences. You can choose your choices, but the consequences of your life will happen as a result of the choices you make. So, if you don't like the consequences of your life, you have to change your choices."

This is a life lesson I've tried to live by my entire life. The consequences of my life are a result of the choices I have made, for good or for bad. While I can seek to blame others, situations, or circumstances beyond my control, I am ultimately responsible for my life, my choices, my emotions, and no one else.

I also understand my choices affect the lives of others, as no one lives on an island of isolation. Every choice I make impacts not only me but my family, my coworkers, my clients and others I am leading in some way.

As a leader, you too must embrace the reality that the consequences of your life are a result of your life choices. You are responsible for your successes and your failures, not others, not your circumstances or your situations. It goes further. Your relationships, career, finances, health and the lives of your followers are affected by the choices you make. So, like the Marines, you need to accept the fact that you are responsible for the choices you make, as well as the choices you failed to make.

In professional sports, teams live or die by their coaching staff. After losing a game, it is interesting to watch the post-game interviews with the coaches. You can tell a true leader when the coach stands before the microphone and takes personal responsibility for the failure of the team. It speaks to the character of the coach if he is willing to take the accountability role seriously before a critical public.

Harry Truman led the United States during a challenging time in our nation's history. He became President at the end of World War II and the beginning of the Cold War. He was responsible for intervening in the Korean War. President Truman understood the importance of personal accountability and his Oval office desk was adorned with a sign that read, *"The buck stops here."* Truman knew there was no need to pass the buck. He made it clear he would be accountable for his actions.

2. *You Must Be Accountable to Your Mentors*

After being accountable to yourself, being accountable to your mentors is paramount to your success as a leader in life. Those who have gone before you, and are actively involved in taking you to the next level, deserve not only your attention and respect but also the right to hold you accountable for what has been asked of you.

A young man started training in our dojo several years ago. He had relocated to the area and was looking for a place to continue his training. He had recently trained in a different discipline than what we taught in our school. We explained to him that what he would learn in our dojo was similar, but there were distinct differences that he would be required to master if he intended to advance in the system we taught.

Every time we would make a correction in his technique, this young man would make an excuse rather than comply. *"That's not how I was taught,"* he would say. Or he might quip, *"My old instructor said this way is better."* One of my favorites was, *"I saw it done this way on a YouTube video and thought it looked really cool."* While the young man had a lot of natural ability, his refusal to submit to the authority of his instructors limited his ability to move up the ranks within our school. Sadly, he ultimately chose to leave the school rather than be accountable for what he was being asked to do by the staff and instructors.

Even great leaders themselves need to be accountable to another mentor. In the dark days preceding the Civil War, America had just elected a new President. Even before he took office, Southern sympathizers were already plotting the assassination of Abraham Lincoln. Elaborate plans were put into motion to kill Lincoln as he traveled by train to Washington DC.

Rather than rely on his own wit and cunning, this soon-to-be leader of the United States put his faith and trust in a man who understood executive protection, Allan Pinkerton. Pinkerton's wisdom came from years of experience as a detective. He devised a plan to disguise Lincoln (not an easy task) and through a series of elaborate ruses, sneaked the President-elect onto a passenger train to elude the assassins lying in wait.

Contrast that with the arrogance of Julius Caesar, who refused the bequests of his wife, Calpurnia, to avoid going to the Forum on the fateful day he was murdered. Believing conquest was within his grasp, Caesar chastised his wife who asked him to feign sickness, only to be stabbed to death on the Capitol steps.

One of King Solomon's often quoted wise sayings is, *"Let him who thinks he stands take heed lest he fall."* Our failure to be accountable to those who have authority over us can eventually lead to our downfall. Many historic battles throughout history could have had a different outcome, and the world we live in would have been drastically different, but for a lack of accountability to those leading the battle. Had Hitler listened to his generals rather than rely on his own twisted thinking, World War II may well have had a dramatically different outcome.

When arrogance trumps accountability, the result is never long-term success. History is full of defeated kingdoms (and failed business endeavors) whose leaders failed to learn the lesson of accountability. The graveyards are full of those who failed to heed the wisdom of Solomon who said, "*There is wisdom in a multitude of counselors (coaches, mentors)."*

In *The 21 Irrefutable Laws of Leadership*, John Maxwell presents the Law of the Inner Circle. This law teaches us that, "*A leader's potential is determined by those closest to him.*" Without an inner circle of men and women to whom you can be accountable, to whom you have given permission to speak into your life, question your decisions and challenge your choices, you will never achieve a Black Belt level of leadership.

3. You Must Be Accountable to the Process

Wouldn't it be great if we could attend a single workshop, listen to one podcast, watch a single video or read a solitary book on leadership and instantly become an expert on the subject matter? Whether it's leadership or any other topic of study, we just don't become an expert on any subject overnight. Until science creates a "smart pill" that instantly boosts our IQ or, like in the Matrix, discovers a means to connect our brains directly to the Internet, we are stuck learning the old-fashioned way.

Learning is a process, and for most of us, it is a process that is ongoing throughout our lives.

In martial arts, learning kata (forms) is a requirement for advancement in most traditional systems. A kata, as previously stated, is a stylized fight sequence to teach muscle memory. Many of the traditional kata have multiple steps (sometimes as many as 30 or more unique movements) in a single pattern and can be quite complicated to learn, even for the seasoned student.

To make it easy for the student, each kata is broken down into segments. A student might be taught the first 3 or 4 movements, and once basic proficiency is achieved, an additional 3 or 4 steps are added. Over time, the entire kata is learned, practiced, and then fine-tuned. After that, the fighting applications to the movements are then taught to each section of the kata, giving the student a deeper understanding of the system's unique fighting elements.

To present the entire kata in a single setting is too much for a student, as the brain can absorb only so much information at one time. Rather than overwhelm the students, we chose to break the training down into smaller "bite-sized" chunks the student could absorb, demonstrate a basic level of competency, and gain confidence as they worked through the mechanics of adding a new skill set to their repertoire.

In our core system, a black belt candidate must be able to show proficiency in 13 distinct kata, as well as a broad assortment of techniques, including punches, kicks, blocks, throws, joint manipulations, joint locks, stances, and movements. The process of earning a first-degree black belt is typically 5-7 years. But that's not the end of the learning.

A first-degree black belt rank in traditional martial arts is not a sign of having arrived; it's a sign that you're now ready to become a serious student of the Arts. There are more katas to learn, more applications to the katas you've already learned, and nuances of the Art that you'll continue to learn for years to come. From there, the journey to 2nd degree black belt is at least 2 years, then another 3 years or more to 3rd degree black belt. It's truly a lifetime of learning, and you'll never learn it all.

So it is with learning to be a leader. In 1993, my dad (a lay pastor) bought me a book from John Maxwell, *Developing the Leader Within You*. That book was my introduction into the world of leadership, but I didn't learn it all from a single book – despite reading it several times. 25 years later, I am still reading, listening to podcasts, watching videos, attending workshops and conferences, participating in mentorship programs and connecting with thought leaders who can help take my level of leadership higher.

In 2011, I met Wayne Nance, the founder of Real Life Management at a meeting where we were both speaking at in Chicago IL. I joined his organization as a Speaker, Coach and Trainer and (as of this writing) have been with RLM for over 8 years. RLM has empowered me to influence countless lives.

In 2017, I joined the John Maxwell Team as a Certified Speaker, Trainer, and Coach and now serve as an Executive Director with the organization. I am also a DISC-certified consultant and am connected with a number of thought leaders who are experts in sales, marketing, influence, leadership, and communications.

The more I learn about leadership, the more I am coming to realize there is always more to learn. Human behavior is complex. Learning how to lead in a variety of settings (and to do so effectively) is something that doesn't happen overnight. The journey of becoming a black belt in leadership mirrors the journey to black belt in martial arts in many respects. It's about learning to be patient in the process – and mastering each technique and strategy you learn along the way.

You see this same process in other settings. TV shows like *American Idol* or *The Voice* go through a process to screen prospective contestants for the Big Stage. Those who get through the initial vetting process then go through a secondary screening process to assure a quality product actually makes it to the Big Stage. The pressure is intense, and those who cannot follow the process, and show proficiency, don't make the cut.

Once the contestants make the actual stage, the process continues. Rehearsals, meeting with coaches and the media, and preparing to "WOW" the judges is a time-consuming process. As they move through the elimination rounds, the process continues, and demands on the contestants who remain increases.

Even after they have won, the process doesn't end. Years later (if they are still in the business), the process of learning and improving doesn't stop. There are always new songs to learn, choreography to master, media events to prepare for and public appearances to attend. The process continues.

Becoming an influential leader who adds value to others and lives a life of significance is a process, not a one-time event. Be patient in the process, and learn the lessons taught along the way.

4. Be Accountable to Your Followers

In mid-November 2017, I found myself blessed with the distinct honor to spend 90 minutes in the office of the Prime Minister of Cameroon. In this private meeting, His Excellency was excited to hear I was a member of The John Maxell Team. He too is a fan of John Maxwell and has read several of his writings. I was privileged to present him with a John Maxwell Leadership Bible, along with a copy of Wayne Nance's book, *The 3-Minute Difference*, introducing him to Real Life Management.

As we talked about the value of leadership and His Excellency's interest in bringing leadership training to his country, we began trading "Maxwell-isms" (famous phrases and quotes by John Maxwell). The entire room burst into laughter when I shared one of my favorite Maxwell quotes, *"If you think you're a leader, and no one is following, you're only taking a walk."*

If you're a leader, then people are following you. They are listening to your words, watching your actions, feeling your emotions and embracing what you value. Leaders have an obligation to be accountable to their followers, for they influence who and what those who follow will become.

Perhaps you have not given this the thought it deserves up to this point. If you are leading others, you are personally responsible for them. What you teach, they embrace. What you demonstrate, they emulate. What you say, they repeat. That places a tremendous burden on you as a leader to be intentional about leading well.

As President of the United States Martial Arts Hall of Fame, I've had the privilege of visiting many martial arts schools here in the United States, the Caribbean, Central America, and Africa. While I have met, and trained with, many quality instructors who take their obligation to lead well seriously, I've also had the displeasure of visiting a small number of schools where this was not the case.

As with any professional sport, you can tell a lot about the quality of the instructor by the performance of his or her students. Not every martial arts instructor truly cares about his students, and that's evident by the fact they are not being led well. The same can be said by watching any individual or team sport. It is not too difficult to tell who is leading well and is committed to being accountable to their followers (students) and who is not.

I found myself in St. Louis as the guest of one of the local grandmasters who was hosting a tournament in the neighboring state of Illinois. As a courtesy, we visited several local schools in the metroplex to make introductions and observe what was being taught in the classroom. In one school, taught by an individual reported to be a highly ranked instructor, students were engaged in sparring (fighting) drills. Yet the students were standing several feet apart – not making contact.

After watching the students engage with each other for several minutes, I politely asked the senior instructor when the students would close the gap and make contact with one another. His response shocked me, "*We don't let the students make contact in class. If they do, and someone gets hurt, they might not come back.*" I left disappointed that this instructor was more concerned about a bruise or a bump than he was about teaching his students how to defend themselves against an attacker. This instructor was not accountable to his followers and was missing an opportunity to teach the practical, real-life applications of self-defense to his students.

True leaders influence the lives of others as positive role models, living out their lives in a manner worthy of being emulated in the lives of others. Being accountable to those who are following means you, as a leader, are adding value to your team. It means you are casting vision clearly, so they can see it, embrace it and pursue it as their own. It also means being intentional about how you lead, knowing that those who are following you will continue your legacy into the future, and they, in turn, will influence other lives as you have influenced theirs. '

The necessity of accountability cannot be overlooked, as it governs our responsibility to ourselves, our mentors, the process and those who are following after us.

Dr. Martin Luther King Jr. is a classic example of a life lived with accountability. Dr. King chose to combat segregation in his era, through a message of non-violent opposition, similar to the approach used by Gandhi who battled for equality in India. Dr. King was accountable to lead himself well and lived a life that inspired others to follow. He was also accountable to his mentors, past and present, honoring their input into his life, taking personal responsibility for his words and his deeds.

Dr. King was also committed to being accountable to the process of non-violent opposition to segregation, choosing to speak the Truth in love rather than take up violence to further his cause.

Despite persecution and hardship, he endured the process, staying the course that led to his famous *"I Have a Dream"* speech that rallied and inspired millions to come to the

Washington D.C. mall in support of desegregation and equal rights.

Dr. King was also accountable to his followers. He led by example, practicing what he preached. As such, he set the standard for his followers to emulate – ultimately bringing about a change in culture, society, and law. His dream that men would not be judged by the color of their skin but by the content of their character became a reality that charted a new course for America and brought freedom and opportunity to generations to follow. (More on Dr. King to follow in subsequent chapters.)

SUMMARY – Level Three (Orange Belt)

"Neither age nor experience matters when it comes to being personally responsible for any and all of my outcomes."
Kory Livingstone

1. You must be accountable to yourself.
2. You must be accountable to your mentors.
3. You must be accountable to the process.
4. You must be accountable to your followers.

The Art of Communication
Chapter Five

The ability to communicate is one of the unique things that sets the human species apart from others in the animal kingdom. While certain species do have a limited ability to communicate, this skill has been uniquely honed to be one of the distinguishing characteristics of humanity. Humans are social creatures, and the ability to communicate thoughts and ideas are key to social interaction.

We communicate in a variety of ways, speech being the most common. We also communicate through our other senses: hearing, sight, taste, and touch. Even our emotions communicate to those around us. We share thoughts and ideas through the written word, music, art, and even culture. As we have advanced as a species, our ability to communicate has gone through an evolution as well, expanding into the electronic world of email, instant messaging, texting and a variety of social media tools such as Facebook, Instagram, LinkedIn, and Twitter.

From the time we were born, we were immersed in a world of language, sounds, tastes, smells, and emotions, all of which shape our identity and how we communicate with others. We learn the language of our culture and how to interact with others to express thoughts, ideas, and emotions.

In school, we learn to read and to write. We learn colors and numbers. We learn mathematics (a communication language all its own), and we may learn how to sing or play a musical instrument, debate, as well as how to draw, paint, sculpt, shape or mold. By the time we have completed high school, we have learned how to communicate using a variety of tools and resources.

Communication can be awkward, at times. At times, we stumble for the right words to say and at other times we say the right thing at the wrong time, the wrong thing at the right time or the wrong thing at the wrong time. Sometimes, we actually say the right thing at the right time. Learning how to make this happen on a more frequent basis can be invaluable in our quest to grow, mature, and achieve significance in our personal and professional lives.

Of all the skills necessary for a leader to see success, the ability to communicate is one of the most essential. If leaders are agents of change, then (in the words of pastor, speaker, and author Andy Stanley) we must learn to *"communicate for a change."*

Communication is defined as the exchange or imparting of information, knowledge, thoughts or ideas. When I was in college, my Business Communications professor made it clear that true communication did not take place until the information the sender was transmitting was understood by the receiver in like manner. In other words, until mutual understanding of the content, and the intent, of the message being shared were comprehended by both parties, communication had not yet taken place.

Miscommunication between two or more people is perhaps one of the most common shortcomings of mankind today, and among leaders it is anathema. If a leader cannot communicate effectively with those who are following, then his or her ability to lead, influence and add value to others is severely limited.

The inability to communicate has individually led to broken relationships, missed opportunities, hurt feelings, and acts of violence. On a global scale, it has led to political and military conflicts going back to the beginning of time. Our failure to communicate, individually and corporately, is perhaps one of the greatest flaws in human design.

But we ALL can learn to be better communicators if we are willing to learn. The Art of Communication is a skill set that leaders must master if they intend to live lives of significance, add value to others and influence others to become positive change agents in their own lives, homes, and communities.

Let's take a closer look at what we need to master as we continue toward becoming Black Belts in Leadership.

1. *Communication Matters*

In 2016, I traveled to the county of Guatemala to lead a team of volunteers from our local church, working with the indigenous mountain people, as well as assisting in an after-school program that provides educational resources for school-aged children and a safe place for children and teens to grow and develop.

I was honored to be asked to teach a series of basic martial arts classes at the after-school center. Over four days, these children would have the opportunity to learn basic stances, blocks, punches, and kicks, as well as some rudimentary self-defense.

The children arrived for the class, excited to learn. It was then I realized we had a communications problem. I could not speak Spanish, and the available interpreter had no martial arts training. The first day was a comedy of errors as I attempted to work with the students, and the interpreter (with whom I had never worked before) attempted to translate what I was saying so these excited participants could understand.

Despite the initial struggles to communicate, the children in the class laughed, yelled, and smiles were the norm throughout the session. At the end of the class, we shared high-fives, hugs and a lot of fist bumps with the participants, and I told them we would do this again tomorrow.

That night, as I went through a mental debrief of the day, I realized that communication matters. Even though I could not speak the language, through an interpreter and by providing visual examples for the students to see, we were able to transfer ideas, concepts, truths. In doing so, I could teach these young boys and girls something they had never learned before.

I thought back to a similar experience while on a trip a few years earlier to the island of St. Lucia. Martial arts legend, Bill "Superfoot" Wallace and I had traveled as guests of honor for the Pitons Open, an international martial arts tournament. Our host scheduled an opportunity for Bill and me to teach a seminar to the teens and young adults who would be competing in the tournament the next day.

When Bill and I arrived to teach the seminar, the room was literally packed with teens and young adults, eager to learn. It was only then we learned that the host, who was unable to attend, had not arranged for a translator. All the participants spoke either Portuguese or French, and only a couple spoke some broken English.

We understood that communication matters, even when you can't speak the language. Bill would demonstrate a striking technique, with me as his partner. He then paused to let the participants practice what they had learned. I borrowed a fellow black belt and demonstrated some basic ju-jitsu. While we could not speak the language, we were able to use non-verbal (mostly visual) communication to help them learn the techniques, strategies, and concepts we were trying to convey.

At the end of two hours, the camp participants were all smiles. We had no idea what they were saying, but the laughter and animated gestures of the participants told us that we had communicated, and connected in a very special way. We posed for a lot of pictures, signed a number of autographs, and thoroughly enjoyed ourselves.

Communication matters, as this is how we share ideas, concepts, truths, and stories. It is how we learn about each other. Communication is how we teach, instruct, and inspire. It's how we influence, add value, and connect with people in an intimate, personal way.

Most people think of communication as simply dialogue. While the ability to speak and use language is one of the primary means of communication, it's not the only means to share thoughts or ideas. Your mannerisms, emotions, actions and non-verbal cues all are "speaking" in some way to those around you.

Communication matters, as this is how values, beliefs. and culture are shared. While in Guatemala, the Team I was with spent two days in the mountains installing cookstoves in the huts of the Mayan descendants who have lived in these remote regions for centuries. For around $200, we could install a stove that took the place of a firepit in the middle of their living quarters, providing a safer (and more convenient) place to cook. It also vented the damaging smoke and contaminants outside the house. This made the living quarters less dangerous for the inhabitants, as they no longer had to inhale these toxic fumes that often led to upper respiratory diseases (especially in the children).

While we could not speak the native language, we were able to communicate through a smile, a touch, or a kind gesture. We showed through the installation of a simple stove that we cared and made their lives, and the lives of their children, better.

The mountain people communicated their joy, appreciation, and gratefulness in many special ways. At one house, tears of joy were shared, at another, the eating of a watermelon. Perhaps the most memorable was an older family who shared a bottle of Coca-Cola with us. We were later told by one of the interpreters that this was the equivalent of sharing a bottle of expensive champagne, as Cola is a luxury that most families simply cannot afford. They may have saved for months or years to acquire a single bottle for a special event or holiday.

> "Miscommunication is perhaps one of the most common shortcomings of mankind today."
>
> John Terry

Communication matters, as this is how we connect as a social creature. Humans are indeed social animals and as such value interaction and connection with others. Sociologists tell us that the power of connection and ability to communicate are essential to the development of a common culture among people-groups and societies. When those values are lost, and the individual members of society stop communicating, connectivity as a people-group is lost, and the decline of society begins.

If you believe communication doesn't matter, try living for a day as the millions of people do around the globe that live life without sight or the ability to hear or speak. To gain a better understanding of the value of communication, read the story of Helen Keller, a blind and deaf girl who overcame extreme odds to become the first deaf person to earn a Bachelor of Arts degree and become one of the 20th century's most noted humanitarians.

If you believe communication doesn't matter, read the incredible story of the POWs who found themselves in the infamous Hanoi Hilton. There they endured unspeakable horrors and torture and found themselves placed in isolation and were prohibited from speaking to other prisoners, and beaten if they did.

These ingenious men developed a means to communicate by tapping on the walls, passing notes from cell to cell, even using sweeping with a cadence to send coded messages (like Morse code). This formed a bond between the men was so strong that this group of POWs refused to leave the Hanoi Hilton until they were able to leave as a group. Communication was essential to their survival.

If you believe communication doesn't matter, try going 24 hours without communicating to those around you. No talking, no gestures, handwritten notes, texting, handshakes, hugs or high-fives. No radio, TV, Internet, Smartphone use, or not even reading the newspaper or a good book.

Communication matters, and if you intend to be a leader in life, you must master the art of communication. Communication is essential to influencing, adding value and inspiring others to live a life of true significance.

2. What You Communicate Matters

"The power of life and death are in the tongue," wrote King Solomon. What we communicate either adds value (life) to others or it takes value (death) from them. From our birth, words have been used to teach, train, inspire, challenge and discipline us. What our parents and others in our formative years spoke into our lives shaped our view of the world, our belief system, our morals and values and the culture we embrace.

What others have spoken into your life has influenced who you are today. What you believe, why you believe it and how you live your life is a direct result of what has been communicated to you from early in your life. Your taste in food, clothing, sports, music, art, and career is in large part influenced by the WHAT your parents and others close to you poured into your life through verbal and non-verbal communication.

The words you speak have power. As King Solomon reminded his readers, the words you speak into the lives of other people either build them up or tear them down. You cannot be a positive influence in the lives of others, nor can you add value to their lives, by speaking words that are not encouraging, inspiring and uplifting.

One of the challenges I faced as a martial arts school owner and instructor was helping the students see the amazing, life-changing potential within. It was especially difficult for those students whose parents, siblings and other family members were constantly bombarding them with negativity. Having been told for years they were stupid, ignorant, clumsy, or worthless, they were now being challenged to see the infinite possibility of greatness within them.

59

It was disappointing to watch students with remarkable ability and talent who simply could not see the tremendous value within themselves, as they had grown up hearing words of negativity, doubt, and limited thinking. Our instructors would do their best to speak positive words of encouragement, inspiration, and no-limits thinking into their lives. We all understood that the seeds of greatness within us are watered by the words we speak and the thoughts we think.

WHAT you say is important, as it sets the tone for your life and the lives of those you are communicating with. *"Think before you speak"* were words of wisdom from my Mom and Dad. For a leader, this could not be truer. If what we say is life or death to the hearer, then we should choose our words wisely.

But WHAT you communicate is more than just words. Dr. Albert Mehrabian (author of *Silent Messages*) conducted several studies on nonverbal communication. He found that **7%** of any message is conveyed through words. **38%** is conveyed through certain vocal elements. A staggering **55%** of all communication takes place through nonverbal elements (facial expressions, gestures, posture, etc.).

If 93% of our communication with others is more than words, then what we are "saying" through our non-speaking (as well as our tone and inflection) is just as important as what we say. When our verbal and non-verbal messaging is not in-sync, mixed messaging result. This can only end in confusion.

"People do what people see," says John Maxwell. Consider the parent who tells their children smoking is bad, yet refuses to quit smoking. The odds are high that this child will follow in their parent's footsteps because actions do tend to speak louder than words. People do what they see modeled before them.

WHAT we say matters, as it communicates not only thoughts but emotions and actions. In "Everyone Communicates, Few Connect", John Maxwell reminds that communication conveys something we know, something we feel or something we do. We cannot truly connect with others unless we understand that communication (and connection) goes beyond mere words.

3. How You Communicate Matters

I started doing TV commercials with my father, who managed an Ivy League clothing store aptly named "Poise-N-Ivy" in the early 1960s. The store was an offshoot of the Arcade Men's Store that provided business attire to the professional and sales community of Fort Smith AR.

Poise-N-Ivy was the "hip" place to buy clothes. It was a novel forerunner of what we would think of today as Men's Warehouse or Joseph Banks. You could be "dressed to the 9's" if you shopped Poise-N-Ivy and it was THE place to shop for style in Fort Smith.

As a young boy in the 4th Grade, I was excited to get to appear on local Channel 40 along with my dad. Playing off the popular "Mod Squad" TV series at the time, the commercials featured "The Ivy Squad", consisting of my dad, a Caucasian, George, an African American, and a young girl – all three decked out in the coolest threads of the day.

I traveled to the TV studio for the first shoot of my illustrious (but short-lived) TV commercial career. My job was to model several items of clothes during a series of commercials that would be shot that night at local Channel 40. Entering the TV studio, I was excited to see the set where the nightly news was broadcast and learned we would be shooting our commercials next to the part of the studio where the weather forecast was given.

My script was simple, comprised of one sentence: *"If I can get bargains like these, think what bargains you can get at the Poise-N-Ivy."* I worked for two weeks, rehearsing that simple sentence, and thought I had nailed it. I marched into the studio, confident, ready for my Big Screen debut – and when the lights came on, the TV director pointed to the huge camera and told me this is where 50,000 people would be seeing this commercial.

The Director set up the shot, the cameras started rolling and somewhere behind the blinding lights someone said "ACTION!" I got about half-way through my lines and flubbed it. We did it again, and once more. It was good, I thought, but my dad, a salesman and a pastor by trade, wanted better.

Dad, my first speaking coach, reminded me, *"John, it's not just WHAT you say, but HOW you say it that matters."* He helped me understand the importance of inflection, emotion, and the value of the presentation was just as essential to communicating as the actual words being spoken.

So, we did one last take, and when the Director said "CUT", he told me that I *"sold that one."* I remember my dad smiling, George patting me on the back and the camera guys clapping for me. For a 4th grader, that was a BIG deal. We shot 4 or 5 commercials that night, and as I changed clothes behind the News Desk (as there weren't enough changing rooms for everyone), I just knew I had arrived. After all, how many 4th graders in Fort Smith, Arkansas were shooting TV commercials with their Dad?

Mr. Cohn, the owner of the clothing store, was the consummate salesman. I would visit the clothing store on Saturdays, and Mr. Cohn and my dad began teaching me how to sell. I was given my own sales book, kept track of my own sales, and had to give a report to either my dad or Mr. Cohn at the end of my "work day".

I got pretty good at learning how to size a man for a suit, shirt, pants, and shoes – as well as how to mix and match shirts and ties with suits to maximize the sales opportunity. Mr. Cohn, like my dad, was a huge believer in the HOW of communication. I learned that subtle changes in tone, inflection, and presence were the difference between selling only a suit, or selling a suit, two shirts, three ties and a pair of dress shoes – not to mention a new belt.

It's not just WHAT you say, but HOW you say it. The HOW of communication affects the emotional connection (or lack thereof) you have with another person, as it can dramatically influence the outcome of WHAT is being communicated. Your HOW actually communicates emotion, passion, influence, and believability.

Consider the simple phrase, *"You shot the dog!"* Change the emphasis (the inflection or the HOW) and this simple sentence takes on several possible outcomes:

- **YOU** shot the dog!
- You **SHOT** the dog!
- You shot **THE** dog!
- You shot the **DOG**!

How many efforts to communicate a thought or idea have been stymied because the HOW and the WHAT did not congeal? The study of neuroscience has found that our brain is comprised of two major regions called the neocortex (evolved) and the limbic (primitive, reptilian) brain.

The neocortex is responsible for sight, sound, hearing, taste, touch, smell, and (in humans) communication. It is also the region of conscious thought. The limbic region is where our emotions, behaviors, and memories reside, as well as subconscious thought.

A few years ago, my wife and I went on a 10-day cruise of the inside passage of Alaska. We left Vancouver and traveled to Juneau and from there to Glacier Bay, Ketchikan, and Skagway. As we drew near Glacier Bay, we were amazed to watch large chunks of ice the size of a two-story house separate from the leading edge of the glacier and crash into the ocean around us.

Only a small segment of the newly formed iceberg was visible above the water. The bulk of this massive chunk of ice floated below the visible surface. Our brains function much the same way. The subconscious seat of our brain, much like the bulk of the iceberg, sits below the surface of the conscious – yet controls our emotions, regulates our body functions and is the gateway to our memories and life experience.

One of the things we have learned from neuroscience is the decision-making process we go through as humans. When faced with a decision, the brain first activates the limbic region, where our memories, life experience, and emotions are stored. Once the brain knows how it "feels" about a decision, the neocortex is then activated so the logical, rational side of our brain can validate what our "feelings" are telling us to do.

The HOW of communication is important, as it is necessary to help the brain make sense of the WHAT. We all want to be with people we know, like and trust. The HOW of communication is essential in achieving that *"know you, like you, trust you"* status with those on your team.

Ben Stein is a gifted economist and brilliant in his field. But he is also remembered for his patented monotone voice in the movie *"Ferris Bueller's Day Off"*. Monotone doesn't provide context, inflection or emotion into a message – so its intent can be lost or misconstrued.

Your emotional status comes through as you communicate and has a direct bearing on your HOW. That is why it is so important that you manage your emotional state rather than allowing your life to be controlled by your emotions. A leader leads by controlling his or her emotions, understanding that the emotional state they exhibit before others will set the tone for HOW a given message is received, interpreted and acted upon.

When it comes to HOW you communicate, there are some specific questions you should pose to yourself to assure that your WHY and your WHAT are in harmony with your HOW.

- Am I being genuine and honest in my communication?
- Does my body language support what I am speaking?
- Is what I am communicating believable?
- Are the emotions I'm displaying consistent with the actual message I'm delivering?

The language of a leader demands that your HOW complements both your WHY and your WHAT. The HOW helps to connect the emotions (WHY) and the intellect (WHAT) so both the conscious and the subconscious parts of the brain are engaged. It stimulates the *"know you, like you, trust you"* connections with those on your team, aligning them to embrace your WHY and to lend their support of your WHAT.

One of the best ways to connect your WHY, WHAT and HOW is through storytelling. From the origins of humanity, people groups passed down their history through the use of stories. When we were children, our parents and grandparents shared stories of days gone by, read us exciting stories and took us to movies where we experienced stories on the big screen. There is something powerful about storytelling in conveying a message, and a leader who can weave his or her WHY, WHAT, and HOW into an effectively woven story can be a communicator who truly connects with others.

A well-told story stimulates not only the conscious. It also engages the subconscious mind, which is the seat of emotions. A story that makes an emotional connection with an audience is a story (and an idea) that is remembered and passed on to others.

In the First Century, Jesus used the power of storytelling to share his message of faith and love, connecting with his audience in a very powerful way. Through the use of common imagery, drawing parallels to everyday life, he connected with his listeners and they understood and embraced his message. Some 2000 years later, there are 2.2 billion people worldwide who are still enamored by his words and claim to be followers of his message.

In ancient Greece, Aesop used the power of storytelling to teach life lessons to young and old. Thousands of years later, we still use Aesop's fables to teach life lessons to our children. The powerful HOW of storytelling enables leaders to effectively communicate their WHY and WHAT more efficiently and coherently.

It's NOT just what you say, but also HOW you say it, that matters!

4. *Clarity and Consistency Matters in Communication*

A leader MUST be clear and concise when communicating. While Porky Pig may be a beloved cartoon character, he would not be considered a role model for effective communication. No one wants to follow a leader who cannot articulate a message clearly and concisely. Leaders who cannot clearly share their vision, communicate their message and inspire others to follow will find themselves walking alone and leading no one.

By definition, clarity is the quality of being easy to see or hear. It is also the sharpness of an image or a sound. For a leader, clarity is an essential skill set that can be learned. Good leaders who also want to be good communicators (and you can't be one without the other) must become lifelong students of the art of communication.

The ability to speak clearly is a learned skill set. It is something that can be taught. Some examples of those who have learned to speak clearly include Zig Ziglar, John Maxwell, Andy Stanley, Joel Osteen, and Paul Martinelli. Gifted communicators use clarity to connect with their audience by being *"easy on the ears"*.

Pau Martinelli tells the story of growing up as a young boy who stuttered. This speech impediment made him the brunt of jokes at school and at home. It also presented him with an opportunity to rise above his current situation to become a gifted orator who inspires audiences around the globe. Paul's transition from a stuttering high school dropout to international business leader is truly an inspirational story of learning the art of communication.

Zig Ziglar, John Maxwell, Andy Stanley, and Joel Osteen are all examples of individuals whose speech and communication style is easy on the ears. Zig Ziglar was well-known for his ability to take complex ideas and concepts and use the power of storytelling to make these things easy to hear, grasp and understand. John Maxwell is a master storyteller and is known worldwide for his clear and concise quips and quotes on leadership and influence.

Andy Stanley and Joel Osteen are consummate storytellers who deliver clear, concise messages to audiences of tens of thousands of listeners who, regardless of education or training, walk away understanding what was said, and how to practically apply it to improve their daily lives. They all practice the art of clear, concise communication and are masters at its delivery. Andy Stanley's *"Communicating For a Change"* shares his focused, yet relaxed style of inspiring, educating and challenging his audience.

For the leader who is pursuing black belt excellence as a leader in life, not only is the ability to be clear and concise in communication a necessity to connect with and inspire their followers, they must model CONSISTENCY in their daily lives.

Consistency, by definition, is firmness of character or constitution. It is also referred to as persistence. My parents defined consistency to me as *"doing the right thing, all the time, even when no one is looking"*.

There is nothing worse than the leader who says one thing and does another. A lack of consistency demonstrates a lack of authenticity with those who are following or observing.

Gandhi was an inspirational leader who was a change agent that transformed a nation. A story is told of a young mother who brought her son to Gandhi for help. For a day and a half, she stood in line with her son to seek the wisdom of this amazing man. When she finally stood before Gandhi she shared her frustration with the fact that her son would not stop eating sweets.

The young boy was, for the most part, a good child. But when it came to sweets, he would lie, cheat or steal to get his hands on sweets. He was a different child when he ate sweets, and despite his mother's pleadings, would not stop eating sweets. His mother begged for Gandhi to speak into the young man's life.

Gandhi paused for a few moments, stared at the young boy hiding behind his mother's sari, and then simply said, *"Come back with your son in two weeks."*

The mother was shocked. *"Two weeks? What kind of response was that?"* she thought. But she agreed and returned two weeks later, with her young son again in tow. After another day and a half of waiting, she again found herself face-to-face with this wise sage.

The mother reminded Gandhi of their prior visit, to which he replied, *"I remember you, and your son."* Gandhi then asked the young boy to come and stand before him. After some coaxing by his mother, the young boy complied and stood before this respected leader.

Gandhi stared at the young boy quietly for several minutes. He then placed his hands on the boy's shoulders, leaned forward to look him squarely in the eyes and said, *"Young man, don't eat sweets anymore."*

Incensed, by his short, simple response, the mother asked why Gandhi couldn't have given this message to her young son two weeks ago rather than requiring them to come back two weeks later. Gandhi's response, *"Two weeks ago, I was still eating sweets. I could not ask this young man to do what I was not willing to do myself."*

Gandhi understood that CONSISTENCY demanded that he be authentic in his actions or his words would ring hollow. Until he gave up eating sweets, he could not in good conscience ask someone else to do likewise. Any leader who wants to live a life of influence and achieve a legacy of significance must see to it that words, feelings, actions, attitudes, values, and convictions align and are lived out consistently, with genuine authenticity.

Growing up, I remember seeing people speak at various venues and at times thinking, *"I don't believe what he (or she) is saying."* At the time, I could not explain the feeling but knew something wasn't right and the message rang hollow.

When words, feelings, actions, attitudes, values, and convictions do not align, the words spoken by a presenter fail to convince, convict, challenge or inspire. There is a PASSION that is almost tangible when a speaker shares an idea or a thought that is CONSISTENT with what he or she believes and lives out on a daily basis.

The power of a clear, concise message that is delivered from an individual with genuine authenticity – consistent with how he or she believes and lives life – is a MUST for any leader who wants to live a life of influence and leave a legacy of significance.

SUMMARY – Level Four (Green Belt)

"Wise men speak because they have something to say.
Fools because they have to say something."

Plato

1. Communication matters.
2. What you communicate matters.
3. How you communicate matters.
4. Clarity and consistency matters in communication.

Leadership is KINETIC
Chapter Six

I remember learning about energy, starting with an introduction to physics in the eighth grade. Mrs. Hill, my science teacher, gave us a series of experiments to learn about various types of energy, including one that involved a Slinky.

For those of you who haven't ever seen or played with a Slinky, it is essentially a large coiled spring of thin, flat wire that was all the rage back in the 1960s and 70s. TV commercials would tout this amazing toy that *"walked down stairs, alone or in pairs, and made a slinkity sound. A spring, a thing, a wonderful thing, everyone calls it Slinky."*

My classmates and I performed a series of experiments to understand the difference between POTENTIAL and KINETIC energy. The Slinky was a classic tool to demonstrate this and made learning a lot of fun, too. If physical science isn't your thing, then let me give you a quick PhySci 101.

POTENTIAL energy is energy that is stored up within an object that has not yet been released. Wind the spring inside a grandfather clock and you are creating potential energy — waiting to be released. The energy held within the coiled spring has the POTENTIAL to be released when given the opportunity.

KINETIC energy is energy in motion. Start the pendulum on that grandfather clock and the stored (POTENTIAL) energy is then released (or converted) into KINETIC energy. Stretch a Slinky out and release it, and it wants to snap back into its original shape.

In our Science class, we would take our Slinky and set it at the top of a flight of stairs. We would then lift the top part of the Slinky and drop it toward the step below. The Slinky would uncoil and as it dropped to the next stair, it would automatically continue to cascade from step to step until it reached the bottom of the stairwell. This simple device kept us entertained for days, as we would experiment with varying ways to release the stored (POTENTIAL) energy within the Slinky to create KINETIC energy.

Within each of us are gifts, talent, and abilities that have the POTENTIAL for greatness. Yet the most talented among us will never achieve greatness if that talent remains untapped, unused. Leadership MUST BE KINETIC, as **Leadership is an ACTION**!

In martial arts, KINETIC energy is an essential element that is learned early on. Why? Movement is necessary when you are fighting an opponent. One of the first things we taught new students was the stances we used in our system. We focused on the importance of foot placement, the tensing of the muscles in the legs and the core, storing that energy, creating the potential for explosive movement (kinetic energy) on demand.

We taught similar techniques for blocking, redirecting, striking, kicking, throwing or trapping an opponent. Learning how to leverage the potential energy within the human body was a key component of learning to fight and defend oneself. We would train not only for strength but for quickness – developing the muscle's ability to leverage both strength and speed for tactical advantage when facing an opponent.

It has been said that the start of any journey begins with a single step. You don't have to be good to start, but you do have to start to be good.   As it is in martial arts training (as with any endeavor in life), engagement is required in order to see success.   Even Napoleon Hill's classic, *Think and Grow Rich*, required more than just thinking for riches to come – it required action. That's kinetic.

As a child, you may have played the game, "Follow the Leader."   On the playground at school, we would take turns leading others on a creative journey over and under monkey bars, running in between the swings, jumping out of swings, running over the see-saws. The more adventurous the leader, the more fun we had.

How much fun would "Follow the Leader" be as a game if the person assigned to lead simply stood still and did nothing. It would not take very long before those who were following either picked someone else to be the leader, or they went on to do something else with their time and energy. There's a lesson in kinetic leadership here:

No Action = No Leadership

LEADERSHIP IS ACTION. It is the release of gifts, talent and abilities in you and in others to achieve a common goal or objective.   LEADERSHIP MUST BE KINETIC or it is NOT leadership. Leaders who aren't leading are not leaders.

There are four key components of kinetic leadership that all black belt leaders in life practice:

1. *Leaders must lead. They must take decisive action.*

Once you have determined your goal or intended destination and formulated a strategy or action plan to get you from Point

A to Point B, there has to be a point in time when you say "Go". You have to take decisive action.

I remember as a child watching my parents plan for our summer vacation. We didn't have a lot of money when I was growing up, so my Mom and Dad typically planned a trip every other year, taking my sister and me to a destination location that would create a lasting memory. They would talk to us about where we were going, what we would do once we got there, and strategize with us about what we should plan to do to pass the time while we drove to our destination.

At some point, the talking and planning had to come to an end and kinetic action had to take place. Bags had to be packed, games, toys, and books for the road trip selected, and hotel reservations were made. The car had to be fueled and loaded and a day was chosen for the journey to start and end. (Even in the planning stage, action steps were required.)

How much fun would a trip to Six Flags be if you simply talked about what you were going to do and never took action? You packed your bags, loaded the car, climbed in the seat, locked the door and put on your seatbelt, then just sat there and never started the car. Sounds like an exciting vacation to me, huh?

Yet how many people will have an epiphany, a moment of creative genius, but never act on this brilliance? How many individuals who are put in charge are never able to get their Team across the finish line because they can't get past analysis paralysis and make a conscious decision to simply take action – to do something?

It has been said that the richest place in the world is the graveyard. Why? Therein lies the books that were never written, songs never sung, businesses never launched, movements never started, inventions never created, and lives that were wasted for lack of action. Regrets fill the graveyards, due to a lack of decisive action.

One of the most important decisions a leader has to make is when to take action. All the best-laid plans of mice and men are for naught if they are never implemented. Alexander the Great, Napoleon Bonaparte, Joseph Stalin, Genghis Khan, and Adolph Hitler are all remembered (for good or for evil) as men of action. Their battles and conquests are remembered in the history books not just for their planning, but their decisive action. The expansion of their empires across the globe would not be remembered, analyzed or studied were it not for kinetic action — decisive implementation of their plans of global conquest.

In martial arts, students are continuously trained in a variety of fighting techniques. Part of that study is learning to see and recognize opportunities to seize a tactical advantage over your opponent. Indecision is often the difference between victory and defeat in battle (whether for sport or a life and death struggle).

Whether it is karate, taekwondo, judo, BJJ, boxing or mixed martial arts in the ring, decisive action is a necessity. All the training in the world will do no good to the competitor who fails to seize the moment and take kinetic action. A momentary drop of the hand, a shifting of the body into an awkward (or strategic) position, a response to a feint or a misstep can all become tactical advantages to the competitor who springs into action.

Emmitt Smith, a former running back for the Dallas Cowboys, is a classic example of decisive action. In the NFL, the best of the best gather on a field of combat to test their skills before sold-out crowds of raving fans. As Emmitt would take a handoff or a pitch, he was constantly watching the field in front of him, studying the action taking place in front of him, looking for that brief opportunity to explode through a hole or take advantage of a defensive player's poor position.

Cutting and weaving, pausing and sprinting, Emmitt was an amazing example of a leader who took decisive action on the field, ultimately entering into the NFL record books. He was known for his patience in the backfield, waiting for the play to develop. Once he saw the pathway open, even if for the slightest moment, he was decisive in his actions – and is known as one of the greatest running backs not only in the Cowboys history but the NFL as a whole.

The same can be said for historic athletes in other sports. Men like Michael Jordan, Tiger Woods, Mario Andretti, Peyton Manning, Tom Brady, Jack Nicklaus, Ozzie Smith, Chuck Norris, Royce Gracie, Bill "Superfoot" Wallace – all were men of decisive action who have become legends in their sport.

Leaders MUST lead, or they are not leaders. Leadership is kinetic.

2. *Leaders must live out what they believe*.

I have taught self-defense classes to thousands, young and old, not only here in the United States, but in the Caribbean, Central America and Africa. Teaching others how to be situationally aware so they can avoid trouble, or fight back when escape is not an option, has been a rewarding endeavor for more than two decades.

When I teach rape and assault prevention on college campuses (and to women's groups), I often bring with me some pine boards, cut into 12" x 12" squares. There is something empowering about learning to break a board, and teaching women how to channel their strength and focus into a single point on the board really boosts their belief in themselves.

I was invited to one particular campus by a couple of sororities after a series of rapes had taken place on the university grounds. About 75 young ladies poured into the student center for a 2-hour class to teach them to recognize and avoid situations that put them at higher risk of assault, and how to fight back if they were attacked. As in most of these classes, the girls were unsure of themselves, not knowing what to expect, or whether or not they could fight off a male attacker if confronted.

I recruited a couple of guys from a local martial arts school both soldiers in the military, to be my Ukes (training partners), and spent some time before the class demonstrating what I would be teaching and what I wanted them to do as simulated "attackers". I am not sure they realized what they were getting themselves into when the first

> "Leaders who aren't leading aren't leaders."
>
> John Terry

volunteered (or their instructor "volunteered" them for me), but they were good sports – and appreciative of the opportunity to help empower women who were being targeted on a local college campus.

After about 45 minutes of reviewing common sense things the girls could do to minimize their risk of becoming a victim, we got into the practical aspects of fighting back. Needless to say, things got INTENSE pretty quickly. At first, the girls were a bit timid and shy as these hulking guys would choke them, grab them, or pick them up and attempt to carry them out of the student center. But as one after another freed themselves from their attacker, the mood in the room went from *"I can't"* to *"I can"*. These girls could not wait for their turn to apply what they were learning, and the room was filled with cheering and screaming as each girl became more and more confident in her ability to defend herself.

Our 2-hour session lasted 3-1/2 hours, as the girls didn't want to leave. They kept asking for an "encore". We concluded with a board breaking session (much to the delight of the Ukes, who were tired from being pummeled over and over by these very intense young women). As the girls broke some boards, using their hands, elbows, knees, and feet – the roar of the crowd was almost deafening. I almost wanted to call Campus Security before I dismissed, and told these young women as much, as they were fired up about fighting back and taking back their campus, and I feared for any young man out walking the grounds that night.

The transformation that took place in the minds of these girls is something that HAS to take place in the minds of any black belt leader in life. ***You have to live out what you believe***. These young women reached down deep inside themselves, found something within they may not have known was there before. They left with a walk of confidence...a belief in themselves they would live out from that day forward. As leaders, we must do likewise. We must live out what we truly believe, as that is the mark of authentic kinetic leadership in action.

James was a leader in the first-century Christian church. One of his teachings to his followers was that *"faith without works (action) is dead."* He was reminding early converts to

Christianity that they must live out what they believe. James also challenged them to be *"doers of what they believe (The Word), and not just hearers only."*

In the opening of the movie, *The Three Musketeers*, the Musketeers are being disbanded, as part of an orchestrated effort by the Cardinal to overthrow King Louis and take control of France. The Musketeers were loyal to the King and pledged their very lives to defend the Kingdom. As the movie progresses, we see three Musketeers who put action to their loyalty, risking life and liberty to prevent an unholy alliance between the Cardinal and England, and halting an assassination attempt on the King.

We see a real-life example of kinetic action in Alexander's Greek army. Alexander the Great's men believed in his destiny to conquer the known world and followed him to the ends of the earth. In the Torah, the Israelites believed in a man named Moses and followed him to the Promised Land of Canaan. In more recent times, the people of Germany believed in a madman named Adolph Hitler and followed him on a quest to conquer the world and establish a 1000-year Aryan global kingdom.

George Washington, Abraham Lincoln, Mahatma Gandhi, Nelson Mandela, Martin Luther King, Jr. all brought about transformational change to a nation by living out what they believed. Washington was instrumental in forming a new nation, while Lincoln is credited with the reunification of North and South. Gandhi and Mandela brought peace and reconciliation to India and South Africa, and Dr. King inspired a civil rights movement that unified the races.

Leaders are men and women of vision. They see before others see, and they believe before others believe. But as

James told his young followers in First Century Jerusalem, if there is no kinetic action to what you believe, those transformational ideas will never come to life. You must live out what you believe if you want others to believe and live it out in their own lives as well.

3. *A leader's action must be duplicatable.*

If others cannot do what you do, you will act alone. One of the responsibilities of a true leader is to lead in such a way that others can follow and see success as well. If your followers find the journey too difficult, or the course of action something they can't participate in or duplicate, you'll soon find yourself traveling solo.

Remember John Maxwell's quote from earlier, "*If you think you're leading, and no one is following, you're only taking a walk.*" Those who are following you must be able to do what you do either because it is something they can do on their own or something you can train them to do. Duplicated effort multiplies your results.

Every civilized culture has had some form of a codified fighting system, either for military purposes, civilian defense, or both. Training in any martial arts system can be simply described as predictable response training. The origins of karate can be traced back to the island of Okinawa, where a fighting system was codified in an attempt to protect oneself against pirates and thieves.

As there were no video cameras to record the fighting steps in response to a threat, the founders of karate combined a series of techniques into a pattern (or form) known as kata. Practitioners would learn these katas (much like learning a dance), as well as the bunkai (application or analysis) of these movements to build muscle memory so these responses became almost instinctive.

The idea was to make the learning of self-defense techniques simple and duplicatable. As students would memorize each kata, they were learning predictable response training. Whether an assailant would attack from the front, rear or from the side, a choke, grab, bear hug, or weapons attack, the student had learned a series of defensive steps to fight back. Modern fighting arts and today's military training in every civilized nation around the world, all follow a similar model.

As leaders, we must take a similar approach to train those who are following. Just like the Sensei is teaching his students to fight and defend themselves, a leader is teaching his followers how to effectively perform the skills necessary to bring an idea to life, achieve a specific goal or arrive at a stated destination. The steps in the process must be clearly defined and demonstrated.

The planning process for a leader (and the team) must not only be to define the desired result but to also outline the steps in the process. The implementation of applicable training is required to assure those on the team can perform each step efficiently and effectively. Not only must each step be outlined, but those on the team also need to understand the bunkai (the "Why") this steps or series of steps, is important.

4. A leader's action must be consistent with his or her values and convictions.

Integrity is defined as congruency between your words and your deeds. Andrew Carnegie once noted as he got older, he listened less to what people had to say but watched more closely to what they did. Speaking as a leader is easy; living as a leader is hard. When there is a disconnect between "*do as I say*" and "*do as I do*", your ability to lead will be limited, and you will ultimately find yourself walking alone.

At the beginning of the Civil War, Union and Confederate troops met at what would be known as the Battle of Bull Run. In the early stages of the Civil War, troops wore the colors of their state militia, sometimes blue and sometimes grey. It was difficult to tell friend from foe. Orders were given by inexperienced officers and were questioned by inexperienced soldiers under their command. The Union troops were confident they would fight a single battle, demoralizing the Confederate troops so severely the War would be over and the Union reunited.

The Union Army advanced, putting the Rebel troops on the run. As they began to retreat toward Henry Hill, the scattering troops saw a man on horseback, General Jackson, ride to the top of the rise, in full view of the approaching Union troops, in an effort to show his men he was unafraid and rally them to action. In plain view of opposing forces, Jackson literally dared the Union troops to shoot him from his horse as he rode to and fro at the top of the rise.

The retreating Confederate troops saw this act of bravado, and it turned the tide of the battle. The legend of "Stonewall" Jackson was born, and the Confederates turned what should have been an overwhelming defeat into a victory for the South. While President Lincoln had hoped for a quick and decisive victory, General Jackson lived out what he believed, his values and convictions on display for all to see, His leadership rallied a ragtag group of misfits to defeat an overwhelming force, ultimately plunging the United States into a bloody civil war that would last for several years.

At the close of World War II, the oratory of Adolph Hitler that had once rallied a nation to take on the entire world began to fade. The hypnotizing speeches that inspired tens of thousands to take up arms against the West were no more. Actions of the Fuhrer had not aligned with his rhetoric, causing even those in Hitler's inner circle to question, and turn from, his leadership. Abandoned and virtually alone, Hitler took his own life while hiding in a bunker, even as Western troops swept into Berlin, putting an end to the Third Reich and rescuing thousands held in Nazi death camps.

Two different leaders; two different outcomes. In each of these examples, the values and convictions were ultimately put on display by the actions taken by the leader, for good or for evil. General Jackson, by living out what he believed, rallied troops to his side, and to the cause of the South, and won the admiration and respect of men on both sides of the conflict. Hitler, who claimed to stand for all that was good in Germany ultimately brought his nation to shame and ruin.

Our core values define who we are and what we believe. Our values define our convictions, those absolutes in our lives that are non-negotiables. Those absolutes will find their way into how we lead others, as our actions cannot remain inconsistent with our core beliefs for long.

Who you are will ultimately define what you do, how you do it, and why you do it. That *"who you are"* moment will be a revelation of what you value, what you hold dear, your core convictions, and the true motivation and desire of your heart. Once those around you experience that revelation of the *"true you"*, this will be a determining factor in whether others will follow you any further.

In high school, I had the opportunity to perform in a musical adaptation of "*Hello Dolly*". I was selected to portray the role of Rudolph Reisenweber, the maître d' of the Harmonia Gardens Restaurant. Knowing little about the character, or the movie in general, I did not feel I could do the character justice without understanding who he was and what his role meant for the plot of the movie.

I watched the movie several times, and even met with a couple of restaurant owners, asking them to explain the role of a Head Waiter and what would be expected. By learning what the core values and convictions of a head waiter would be, I could better "live out" those values through my actions onstage. To me, and the audience who watched (and laughed at our antics), Rudolph came to life on the stage because I took the time to learn to, think, speak, and act as a maître d' should, including the famous scene known as the "Waiter's Gallop".

What was in me was able to come out of me, making the character real. Many in our cast, including those who had the major, starring roles, did an incredible job of not only learning their lines but the essence of the characters they were playing. We performed to a packed-out auditorium for several nights, including a night when we thought the snow and ice would cancel the production.

While it was only a high school play, it taught a valuable life lesson to those of us who performed. ***You cannot bring a character to life that you do not have inside you.*** Will Smith's portrayal of Muhammad Ali, Gary Oldman's reprisal of Winston Churchill during World War II, and Heath Ledger's role as Batman's arch enemy, The Joker, were all a result of these actors taking the time to research the character they were tasked to replicate on the Big Screen and internalize the essence of who they were.

The problem for me in the High School play was the accent. I'm from the South, and while my accent isn't overly *"Southern"*, it certainly isn't Prussian, which was the country of origin for Rudolph Reisenweber, the maître d' of the Harmonia Gardens Restaurant. The essence of who I was crept into my conversation, despite my best efforts to stay in character. I jokingly told the Director that I was from Southern Prussia when my *"twang"* manifested.

If you have ever done any acting, you know you can stay in character only so long. *Even the greatest Hollywood legends will tell you that.* At some point, the *"true you"* comes out – and if there is an inconsistency between that and the character you're portraying, that character becomes fake, non-believable, and loses credibility with the audience. The same applies to you as a leader.

If you want to lead like a black belt, your actions must align with your core values, and be evidenced by your convictions, as lived out in your daily life. This is a true man (or woman) in the mirror moment that a real leader pauses and considers on a regular basis. If you want to lead, and lead well, there must be harmony between the thoughts you think, the words you say and the actions you put on display for others to see.

The James Allen classic, *As a Man Thinketh* echoes the wise sayings of King Solomon. As a man thinks, he speaks and does. It is an inescapable law of leadership. John Maxwell says you cannot lead from a place you have not been. A leader MUST lead from his (or her) values and convictions as these are the essence of who the leader truly is. You cannot consistently lead from an area of weakness or an area that is inconsistent with your core values, beliefs, and convictions.

Leaders must be kinetic; men and women of action. Until you take action as a leader, taking the initial risk, you only have standers and not true followers. Leaders lead, and that requires kinetic action.

SUMMARY – Level Five (Blue Belt)

"Do you want to know who you are? Don't ask, ACT!
Action will delineate and define you."
Thomas Jefferson

1. Leaders MUST lead. They must take decisive action.
2. Leaders must live out what they believe.
3. A leader's action must be duplicatable.
4. A leader's action must be consistent with his or her values and convictions.

Leaders Exhibit Boldness
Chapter Seven

Boldness is defined as *"not hesitating or fearful in the face of actual or possible danger or rebuff; courageous and daring; beyond the usual limits of conventional thought or action."* (Dictionary.com)

Children can teach us a LOT about boldness. Growing up, I watched Art Linkletter on TV. Art was the emcee on a show entitled *"Kid's Say the Darndest Things"*. It was and still is, (in my humble opinion) one of the classic family-friendly comedy shows of all time.

You never knew what would come out of the mouths of these young boys and girls in this hilarious show, and many spoke with candor and boldness that added to the show's unique format, and its success. Over the years, many a parent (and the emcee) was embarrassed and amused by the musings of these children on TV.

With 6 children, and now 3 grandchildren, I have had my own share of *"Kid's Say the Darndest Things"* moments over the years.

Around the age of 4, my middle son, Jordan, began to demonstrate a knack for telling jokes. He quickly went beyond simple "Knock, Knock" jokes to telling some elaborate stories with a humorous ending. Anytime someone would say, *"Hey Jordan, tell us a joke."* he was quick to comply - and always looking for a new story to get a laugh.

His deadpan delivery was hilarious to watch as this chubby-cheeked little boy would stand on a chair or a table, climb up on a stage, or seize any vantage point to command the attention of young and old alike. The size of the audience didn't matter; Jordan was fearless when it came to telling jokes.

When my sister, Tonya, was getting married, I traveled with Jordan (and his older brother, Jonathan) to attend the festivities. After the wedding rehearsal, we went out to eat at a swanky restaurant in Nashville. We sat at a large table in the middle of the main dining room as we began to celebrate this couple's new life together.

Small talk ensued, as we began to share stories of the engaged couple among family and friends. We did our best to keep the volume down out of respect for the other guests in the restaurant. That is until someone asked Jordan to tell a joke.

In a restaurant full of strangers, Jordan stood to his feet at one end of the table and began an impromptu stand-up comedy routine. People around us stopped what they were doing to listen to this straight-faced 4-year old tell a few hilarious stories that had us all laughing. And not just our table, but several of the tables around us joined in as Jordan took the stage and shined.

When he was done, Jordan sat down, as if nothing had happened, and went back to snacking on his plate. Mind you, this was a 4-year old in a public setting with probably 60 or more people around him. No fear, no doubt (and to be honest, no concern for the conversations taking place around him) - Jordan simply demonstrated boldness.

The Merriam-Webster Dictionary further defines boldness as *"a willingness to take risks and act innovatively; confidence or courage."* Boldness is the ability to stand firm, even in the midst of adversity. It is the willingness to "leap from the lion's mouth", as we saw in the movie, *Indiana Jones and the Last Crusade.*

A leader must be BOLD, in word and deed. I've heard John Maxwell say many times that *"Leaders know more, and they go before…"* To take the lead and ask others to follow you requires boldness. This inner confidence in oneself stirs up courage in others to leave the status quo and follow you on your quest toward significance.

Boldness is one of the most visible traits of leadership to those you are leading. It is the inspiration to others to take a risk, dare to do what others say can't be done and to be an innovator. Boldness is a character trait of the world's greatest inventors, as these men and women were willing to challenge the status quo, to dream the impossible dream, and have the confidence to believe the impossible can be achieved.

Where would we be if individuals like Albert Einstein, Leonardo Di Vinci, Madame Curie, Alexander Graham Bell, Nicholas Tesla, Henry Ford, Thomas Edison, Steve Jobs and Bill Gates (to name a few) were not willing to lead with boldness to bring to reality the myths and dreams of man?

Where would we be if individuals like Mother Theresa did not lead with boldness to show us that one person can make a difference in the world, and inspire millions to follow her example of generosity and compassion to what the Bible refers to as "the least of these"?

Where would those who are following your leadership be without YOU? How many projects would be left on the drawing board, never seeing the light of day? How many lives would stay the same without your bold leadership and inspiration to pursue a cause or course of action that transforms the lives of others, adding value in the process?

Boldness is transformational; as it inspires others to attempt what they otherwise might believe is not possible.

1. Boldness transforms you from "I Can't" to "I Can".

Like many kids, I was bullied as a child. Prior to training in the martial arts, I would often go to school fearful of what the day would bring. Would I have to sacrifice my lunch money to buy-off a bully from hurting me on the playground? Would I be able to go to the bathroom or go on the playground without being verbally or physically harassed?

I remember walking into the Karate School where I took my first lessons. I was excited, and terrified, at the same time. At the young age of 13, I was the ONLY teenager in class. The closest person to my age was a young lady in her early 20s. In my mind, I was going from getting beat up by kids on the playground to getting beat up by full grown men and women. At least this young lady was pretty, but she was tougher than most of the guys in the school.

But I took that risk and began to train. I earned my yellow belt, then my orange. I broke my first board, then my first concrete block. I learned how to recognize danger, defuse a bad situation, or defend myself when avoidance was not an option. As I continued to train and advance, my confidence grew. I wasn't afraid to go to school anymore.

Boldness began to bring out that *"I can do that!"* confidence that crept into other areas of my life. My passion to try new things, to explore what I could do, grew with each new accomplishment. I auditioned for a musical and earned a role both as a speaker and a dancer. I began public speaking. I wrote my first book, and then two more. I started a commercial sound company while in college, mixing sound at hundreds of concert and conference venues while still in my early 20s.

With the help of an enthusiastic young partner, he and I built 3 martial arts schools. Together, we trained a number of black belt leaders who now own or help run successful schools of their own. I currently oversee an international martial arts association and have a successful coaching and development company, focused on leadership, communication, sales, team building, and behavioral analytics.

Each of these was a bold step. It took courage to take a risk on a new venture, to invest and re-invest in myself (and others), and to have confidence in myself. We boldly

> "Leaders know more, and they go before..."
>
> John Maxwell

began to believe that anything is possible. I believed, and still believe, *"I can do that!"* and that nothing is impossible for those who are bold, and willing to dream BIG!

I spoke earlier of a martial arts living legend, my friend, Bill *"Superfoot"* Wallace. He retired, undefeated, as the Professional Karate Association's middleweight champion and continues to teach and inspire others to pursue martial arts excellence. But Bill had his own boldness moment when he had to transition his mindset from "I can't" to "I can".

Bill began his martial arts career as an accomplished wrestler and later transitioned to the art of Judo. After a significant injury, Bill was unable to continue his Judo training, so he faced a decision. Give up the martial arts he could no longer do, or take a bold step to do something he had never done before. Bill chose *"I can"* over *"I can't."*

That's boldnes*s!*

He began training in karate, eventually earning his black belt in Shobiashi Shorin Ryu under its founder Eizo Shimabuku in Okinawa. Bill began competing, and winning, and winning, and winning. He quickly became known for his lightning-fast hands and feet. His trademark sidekick has been clocked in excess of 60 miles per hour, earning him the nickname *"Superfoot"*.

Even after multiple hip replacements, Bill continues to impress students and instructors around the globe with his fighting prowess, his flexibility (yes, he can still do the splits) and his passion for passing on his knowledge. *"Superfoot"* continues to inspire thousands to be bold in their training, to believe they can be a better martial artist and to pursue excellence in their training.

As a leader, part of your responsibility is to help those who are following see the possibilities before them. Leaders lead because of experience, expertise, and the ability to see the big picture, They possess the boldness necessary to make the decision, take decisive action and accept responsibility for the outcome.

Many on your Team may have not yet gained this insight. Their decision-making abilities will be limited by a lack of experience, expertise, or their inability to see the big picture. This limits the choices available to them, which can lead to an "I CAN'T" attitude that stifles productivity and achievement.

It is the boldness of a leader, demonstrating confidence in his or her decision-making that helps the Team take a risk and consider options which may seem unworkable at the onset. Remember, leaders know more and leaders go before, setting the example to others this can be done.

If Sir Edmund Hillary had not ascended Mt. Everest, boldly doing what no man had done before, would others follow his lead to summit the mountain? It took a bold leader to inspire others to climb the mountain many said could not be scaled by mortal man.

What is the Mt. Everest you're boldly leading your team to summit?

2. Boldness can be developed in the lives of others.

When I was a school owner, it was amazing to watch young students enter our martial arts studio and develop. These often shy, unassuming young lives were initially fearful at times - as it can be intimidating to walk into a martial arts school as a new student and see high ranking students performing with excellence. Sparring, at times, brought great trepidation as students donned padded gloves, headgear, and footpads for the first time.

As these young students learned the basics of blocking, punching and kicking - and saw that what they were learning actually worked, confidence began to ensue. Boldness was beginning to rise up within them. With each class, they attended, each tournament they participated in, and each rank advancement test they passed, you could see boldness and confidence on display.

What I enjoyed most about this transformation was seeing the positive benefits in the lives of these students as boldness pushed them out of their comfort zone in other areas of their lives. The pursuit of "Black Belt Excellence" in class often carried over into their academic studies, extracurricular activities at school (band, sports, etc.) and more.

Today, these students have excelled in martial arts. Many have also gone on to earn "All State" and "All Region" honors in band; graduated with "Honors" and "High Honors" from high school, earned scholarships to prestigious universities, and performed in school plays or musicals. Others are climbing the ladders of success in business as a result of living an "*I can*" life of boldness.

As leaders, we have the unique opportunity to develop those around us, bringing out the best in them and helping them to see the gifts and talent within they may not yet see for themselves. Investing in their personal development helps to instill confidence and courage, hallmark traits of a life lived with boldness.

Far too many people live below their potential because they don't have a role model pouring into their lives, inspiring them to pursue excellence as they discover and develop their strength zones. Leaders who boldly go before others demonstrate a CAN DO attitude that is contagious. As others come alongside, leaders have the privilege and opportunity to develop them to also become Black Belt Leaders in Life. This brings about transformational change that leads them to live a life of significance.

How many people do you know who have given up? Those who have simply quit trying due to a setback or failure in their lives? Life has thrown them a curveball and rather than keep swinging, they have returned to the dugout. They are no longer playing the game of life.

It takes boldness to keep swinging for the fences, especially when it seems like all you are doing is fanning the air. Leaders are like the coaches who continue to work with their players to make them better, faster, stronger. Because when all the players on the team are better, faster and stronger, the team wins more often. They believe they can win the Pennant, the Playoffs, and even the World Series.

That's boldness!

How many causes have yet to be taken up because no one has had the boldness to step up, speak out, and make a positive difference? It takes bold leadership to take on a cause bigger than yourself but when you do, and you do it well, you inspire others to rally to your cause. Together you can make a difference.

Bold leaders build bold followers, who become bold leaders over time and replicate this process in the lives of others. Boldness is a leadership component that can be developed in the lives of others.

3. Boldness compounds results.

To live a life of significance and to be a transformational change agent requires boldness. Leaders cannot passively lead others. They don't just sit back and hope success will come. Leadership requires action...and action requires boldness.

Rosa Parks was an unassuming African-American who lived during the dark days of segregation in 1950s-1960s America. It was a troubling time when the color of a person's skin often dictated their access to many public accommodations, such as drinking fountains, bathrooms or public transportation.

It was a common practice in many parts of the country during this period of time that African-Americans were required to sit in the back of the bus. Rosa Parks, like Martin Luther King Jr., believed that it was the quality of character and not the color of one's skin, that should judge a person, and that all people were created equal in the sight of God.

Rosa Parks demonstrated an act of boldness taking her seat not in the back of the bus, but in the front. It was a risky move for this mild-mannered African-American woman, but one that would help launch a movement for civil rights that ultimately brought an end to the segregationary practices and violence that marred the 1950s and 1960s.

Today, we have seen this boldness compound. We have seen a growing number of African-Americans rise to prominence in our nation. Our nation elected its first African-American president, Barack Obama. We've seen our first African-American Secretary of State, a number of high-ranking military leaders, political leaders and prominent pastors like T.D. Jakes rise to the national stage. Boldness demonstrated by Rosa Parks, Martin Luther King Jr., and others helped to compound the positive results for African-Americans and other minorities in these United States.

A leader who demonstrates boldness inspires those who follow. This has the effect of compounding the efforts, and the results, of any endeavor this group puts its collective hands to do. As success is realized, it leverages that CAN DO attitude among the individual team members, and the group, that they can achieve greatness with each and every challenge they face.

You clearly see this compounding effect as you look at the history of NASA. With President John F. Kennedy's call in the early 1960s to put a man on the moon before the end of the decade, NASA scientists were faced with a looming challenge - to do what had never been done before by creating technologies that to this point were nothing more than impossible dreams in the minds of a few.

But NASA decided to GO BIG and GO BOLD! Starting with the Gemini and Mercury projects, they began building and testing rockets, spacecraft, and systems that would be needed to put a man into orbit. From there, the Apollo project would stretch the creative genius of mankind as NASA scientists struggled to design and build technologies and systems that would take mankind thousands of miles outside earth's atmosphere to an inhospitable lunar surface, and bring them safely home.

Each step along the way, NASA scientists were required to make bold decisions. To take risks that would put men's lives in peril. To venture into a void that was unknown, with technologies that were untested, all in an effort to make an impossible dream a reality. And in 1969, Apollo 11 touched down in the Sea of Tranquility and Neil Armstrong set foot on the moon. Boldness brought a dream to reality.

We saw boldness compound results during the Apollo 13 mission when an explosion on the spacecraft caused damage to its oxygen supply, and the ship itself, forcing the mission to the moon to be aborted. The impossible challenge now was to get these astronauts home safely. Mission Control had to create a "Plan B" that had never before been considered. Lives were in the balance.

The confidence of this NASA Team, as a result of years of bold decision making, was put on public display. Scientists and engineers worked around the clock to explore every available option to save the lives of these brave astronauts and bring them home safely in a vehicle that was never designed to be used for this length of time. Bold thinking, courageous action, and a CAN DO attitude brought Apollo 13 and its astronauts safely home.

Today, NASA has its sights set on Mars, and beyond. The bold thinking and dare to dream big attitude of these scientists and engineers have brought about technological advances that had revolutionized the world. We are seeing the fictional worlds of Buck Rogers, Star Trek, and Star Wars become reality. Bold leadership brings about bold innovation that is truly world-changing.

As a leader, you may not be called on to make life and death decisions as the NASA Team faced with Apollo 13. However, when you put boldness of thinking and display confidence in action to your Team, you inspire them to have a CAN DO attitude that makes the impossible seem achievable.

4. Boldness is not brashness.

Let me be quick to add that boldness doesn't mean brashness. Even a bold decision requires careful thought and consideration. Many leaders fail the test of boldness when they ignore the importance of thinking through the situation, evaluating the myriad of possible approaches and outcomes, and giving careful consideration to the consequences of their choices.

When my children were young, we took a lot of "mini-vacations" in the family van. As you can imagine with a van full of kids, we looked for opportunities to stop along the way to stretch our legs, take in some scenic sights, and work off some restless energy from hours on the road. We also looked for "teachable moments" along the way to start a conversation that lead to a life lesson moment.

On one particular trip, we were traveling to Branson MO. We had season passes to Silver Dollar City, so it was a trip we made a few times a year. At least one of the kids had to go to the bathroom, so we stopped at one of the many hillbilly-themed tourist traps along the way.

The "general store" sold honey cured ham, candy corn, kettle corn and sodas in a glass bottle. We asked about available restrooms and were directed to the other end of the property. The lady behind the counter smiled as she told my children they would get to use the "double-decker outhouse". A teachable moment was at hand.

Growing up in Arkansas, we were familiar with outhouses. Basically, a hole dug into the ground with a small shack erected around it for privacy. You "did your business" through a hole cut in a wooden seat, adding to what was already collecting (and fermenting) in the ground. Not the most pleasant place to find yourself on a warm, summer day.

This particular outhouse was indeed a two-story structure. Of course, the only working part of the outhouse was the lower section, but at least one of my children initially refused to go in out of fear they might be on the "receiving end" of an upstairs customer using the second story privy.

We all got a good laugh out of this, took some photos of us standing in front of the double-decker, pointing to a sign that said: *"Upstairs closed until we figure out the plumbing."* As we got on our way, we began to talk about the experience, and a boldness conversation ensured.

One of my children noted it was awfully brave of the people who owned this property to have the insight to build a double-decker outhouse so more people could go to the bathroom at the same time. Another commented that, while it may have been innovative and brave to build a bathroom this way, it certainly wasn't well thought out. One of my boys was just glad no one was "pooping" upstairs while he was going to the bathroom.

While humorous, this is a great example of boldness vs. brashness. How often do we act on an impulse to be innovative, creative or explore something new and different without giving any thought to the ramifications of acting on this impulse?

Choices have consequences, and the consequences of our lives are a result of the choices we have made. While it is okay to be bold in your thinking, and decisive in your actions, it is NOT okay to simply make choices without first pausing to give thought to the consequences.

In ancient Israel, history tells of a young boy named David went to visit his brothers, who were at war with the neighboring Philistine army. The Philistine champion, a man named Goliath, railed insults at the Israeli army for days. A giant of a man, he called for a champion of Israel to meet him on the field of battle to fight man-to-man in a winner take all fight to the death.

While the soldiers feared to engage this 9-foot tall seasoned warrior, the young shepherd boy went to the king asking permission to challenge Goliath in battle. David had learned leadership at an early age as he shepherded sheep in Israel. He had been battle-tested, killing both a lion and a bear who had attacked his flock. His years of training in the hill country had developed a boldness and a confidence that made him utterly fearless. With the king's permission, David confronted Goliath.

Even though he was a seasoned warrior, well armed and well protected by his armor, Goliath was unprepared for the sight before him. Rather than sizing up this feisty young challenger, brashness set in. Without giving thought to the weapon David carried, Goliath began to hurl insults and mock this young shepherd boy.

David's boldness came from the victories he had earned through prior conflict, and years of honing his skill with the slingshot he carried. David knew in close quarters combat, he stood no chance against this armed, experienced warrior. But at a distance, David knew he could take out this giant with a single stone.

While the giant in his brashness continued to hurl insults, mocking young David, the Israeli army and the religious beliefs of this people group, David reached into his pouch, placed a stone in his sling and began to twirl the slingshot as he approached. He released the stone, striking the giant in the forehead, stunning him with the force of the blow. Without hesitation, David ran forward and using Goliath's own sword he decapitated this Philistine warrior as both armies looked on.

History tells us the Philistine army fled in fear as the Israeli army pursued them. David went on to be honored by King Saul, marrying the King's own daughter, and eventually becoming King over a united nation of Israel.

While a brash decision might not end as badly for you as it did for Goliath in this ancient story, bold actions taken without due consideration can lead to drastic results.

Engineers rushed to build a suspension bridge several years ago without first considering the effect of the wind on the stability of the platform in gusty conditions. While the plan to build this suspension bridge may have been bold, in their brashness they failed to consider all the pertinent facts and shortly after the bridge's completion, a strong wind began to cause the bridge platform to rock and sway violently, eventually resulting in the collapse of the bridge.

Brashness is a form of arrogance. By definition, according to Merriam-Webster, being arrogant is *having or revealing an exaggerated sense of one's own importance or abilities*. How often do we see brashness displayed in the sports world, or in politics? For example, the boxer or MMA fighter who thinks too highly of himself or the celebrity athlete in football or basketball whose arrogance is put on display every time he is interviewed. How about the politician who is overly confident in his or her own self-worth? Brashness or arrogance can be a dangerous thing. It is self-seeking, reckless and ultimately harmful to the individual and those around them.

Leaders who are bold are bold for the sake of the cause. They seek the betterment of others and are not self-serving to enhance their own position, power or ego. Leaders who are brash are more about their own accolades, position, and power.

Contrast that prideful display of brashness to the boldness of a real leader. Winston Churchill displayed boldness as he rallied a nation to withstand the Nazi attempts to invade and destroy their nation. His battle cry, *"We will never surrender..."*

became a tipping point that rallied a nation to rise to the occasion and stand against the onslaught of an enemy focused on their destruction.

Boldness is an integral character trait for a Black Belt Leader. You cannot passively lead, and lead effectively. The bold example you demonstrate before others can inspire them to also dig a little deeper, encouraging them to get out of their comfort zone and stretch for the next level of success.

American author and theologian, Mike Yaconelli, summarized boldness when he said, *"Boldness doesn't mean rude, obnoxious, loud, or disrespectful. Being bold is being firm, sure, confident, fearless, daring, strong, resilient, and not easily intimidated. It means you're willing to go where you've never been, willing to try what you've never tried, and willing to trust what you've never trusted. Boldness is quiet, not noisy."*

SUMMARY – Level Six (Purple Belt)

**"Boldness isn't something you are born with.
You either choose it, or you don't."**
Mike Yaconetti

1. Boldness transforms you from "I Can't" to "I Can".
2. Boldness can be developed in the lives of others.
3. Boldness compounds results.
4. Boldness is not brashness.

The Essentialness of Equipping
Chapter Eight

My dad, at the ripe young age of 84, rebuilds and repairs antique clocks. My former bedroom in my parents' home has been converted into a clock repair workshop. Any time I visit, my dad takes me into his office to show me some of the clocks he is working on. Clocks, sometimes more than a hundred years old, housed in intricately carved wooden housings of all shapes and sizes, adorn his workshop...and all in various stages of repair.

One clock, he explains, needs a new gear. In another clock, he points out, the mainspring has been too tightly wound, causing the motor to seize up. Yet another, he says, simply needs a good cleaning. In the corner, a box he picked up at an estate sale contained a housing, gears and a motor. He was rebuilding this clock from the available pieces, and hand filing gears to the precise size to replace gears either broken or missing.

For Christmas a few years back, he presented me with a Grandfather clock he had picked up at a garage sale, refinished the housing and rebuilt the motor. It was gorgeous and remains a showpiece in our home's dining room. We also have a late 1800s vintage wall clock which he also rebuilt, including a new faceplate. It is hanging on the wall in my downstairs "Man Cave" and is reminiscent of what you would see when watching "High Noon" or other classic Western movies.

My dad learned this very unique skill set from an older gentleman who used to work on the grandfather clocks in the furniture store my dad worked in for nearly 3 decades. As their friendship developed over the years, this older man began to share his knowledge with my dad. He informed my dad he had learned this trait from his own father, who had learned it from his father, going back several generations.

This older man and his wife had no children of their own, so to honor his commitment to passing on what he had learned, he took my dad under his wing (adopted him, so to speak) and began to teach him the intricacies of clock building and clock repair. Now years later, my dad has clients in several states and continues to perpetuate the life and legacy of a skilled artisan who took the initiative to impart wisdom and knowledge through equipping.

I was with John Maxwell in the spring of 2017 when he shared with us that one of our responsibilities as a leader was to work ourselves out of a job. As we lead others, we have an obligation to equip and train them to learn what we know, add to that knowledge, and empower them to do the same with others.

Knowledge not shared is ultimately wasted. When the ancient Library at Alexandria burned, hundreds of years of accumulated knowledge were lost. Knowledge must be passed on to have lasting value, and the wisdom of how to use that knowledge must be passed on as well lest the knowledge is corrupted or used for the wrong purpose.

For a leader, equipping your followers is an essential element to helping your team achieve its goals, dreams, and vision. One of the major goals of an effective leader is empowering those who follow to also become leaders, and that requires equipping. You cannot create future leaders who do not know what you know, how to do what you do and how to become who you are.

In martial arts, equipping is an essential element of training. A style or system was codified by a Founder, who in turn began to take students under his watchful eye...imparting knowledge and wisdom. Over time, these students became senior students (disciples) who intently studied the teachings of their Instructor so they could master the Art he taught.

When the time was right, the Founder empowered these disciples to begin to pass on to other students in their school what they had been taught, duplicating and expanding the influence of the Founder. Until his death, he continued to pour into the lives of his senior students so they could continue to perpetuate his teachings and legacy to future generations.

Today, tens of thousands of students, training in hundreds of styles and systems, continue this same journey. The equipping process has allowed for the proliferation of martial arts worldwide, all while remaining true to the origins of the Founder's techniques and applications. Martial arts schools continue to put out black belts, many who go on to open successful schools of their own, expanding the influence of the martial arts worldwide and perpetuating the Arts.

1. Equipping Inspires

Few things inspire success more than equipping. My oldest son, Jonathan, began taking apart lawn mowers and tinkering with small engines when he was around 5 years of age. Seeing his interest, his grandfather began to teach him about tractors and engines. He taught him how to use tools, diagnose mechanical problems and to run a machine shop. By the time he was in high school, Jonathan was repairing motorcycles, lawn mowers, tractors, and automobiles.

Because Poppa Jim took the time to teach Jonathan, passing on his knowledge and experience, Jonathan quickly gained a knack for diagnosing mechanical problems and identifying solutions. Shortly after graduating college, he went to work for a Suzuki shop as a mechanic and later started working for a small engine repair company who worked on motorcycles, watercraft, and lawn mowers and also did small engine repair before opening his own shop a few years later.

Looking for a new challenge, he interviewed with Glad Manufacturing for a mechanic's position and amazed the plant managers with his ability to understand the mechanical operations of machinery he had never before seen and was hired. So impressed were they with his work, he has been promoted several times. Today, he manages a crew of maintenance professionals who keeps the machinery operational and continues to minimize downtime through their efficiency.

The equipping of Poppa Jim and others who have expanded Jonathan's knowledge of mechanics have inspired him to believe he can take on any and conquer any mechanical problem.

I am inspired by the Armed Forces, especially those who rise to become members of one of the Special Forces teams. These dedicated men and women epitomize the concept of inspiration through equipping. Trained by those who have come before them, these men and women become the BEST because they are trained by the best. With each successive generation of graduates, who learn from the ever-increasing pool of knowledge, wisdom, and experience, the graduates of these Special Forces are inspired to believe they can take on, and conquer, any enemy combatant, in any type of conditions, anywhere in the world.

Facing (at times) overwhelming odds, we continue to see bravery on display as missions, such as the killing of Osama Bin Ladin. We've read the book or seen the movie, *Lone Survivor*. These men and women inspire those who serve alongside them, and those who come behind them, to pursue excellence and live a life of significance as they fight for a cause greater than themselves.

I have been privileged to watch, and on occasion train with, a handful of elite members of the Israeli Defense Forces. I have seen firsthand how the equipping they receive inspires them to be bold in the face of danger and turn the odds in their favor, despite overwhelming opposition. They understand the value of equipping and drill that into those of us who've been privileged to train alongside them, and we walk away more confident, better prepared, and inspired as a result.

A leader who wants to motivate those who follow must make equipping an integral part of the leadership journey. As you take the time to pour your knowledge, wisdom, and experience into those on the journey with you, you inspire them to believe they can do more, and be more, than they are today.

The leader who will not equip others is failing as a leader. When position and prestige become more important than empowering those you are leading to grow and achieve success, that leader is a failure. True leadership is not about position, prestige or power - it is about adding value to others, equipping them with what they need to see success, and empowering them to duplicate this process in the lives of others.

2. Equipping Informs

I shared with you earlier, as a young teen training in the martial arts, I found kata fascinating. Kata is a series of movements intended to simulate a fighting sequence or a series of fighting sequences. It is intended to build muscle memory through what I refer to as "predictable response training". At its essence, kata is stylized fighting against an imaginary opponent or opponents.

My initial enthusiasm with kata was learning the movements and patterns. Not only was this a requirement for rank advancement, but I found the mental focus and physical aspects of kata to be a challenge. Stances, transitions, blocks, parries and punches performed in a stylized fashion (or pattern), to me, was fun.

As I rose through the ranks and began training with several instructors, my understanding of kata grew. There were subtle fighting elements in kata I had yet to learn. Hidden in these movements were effective fighting strategies that worked in real life situations. Learning more only deepened my passion to want to learn more, and I began to explore how the various movements in kata could be used in other self-defense settings.

A byproduct of my kata training was an improvement in my fighting. The more I trained in kata and studied its movements and applications, the more my eyes began to be open to seeing these opportunities during sparring or self-defense class. The information I received through kata-based training equipped me to perform at a higher level in other areas of my training and to become a better practitioner of the arts and a better instructor to our students.

As I previously shared, the CEO of John Maxwell's companies is Mark Cole. Over 17 years ago, Mark began his leadership journey traveling with John Maxwell. He has had the privilege of traveling around the globe with John Maxwell and witnessed firsthand the power of transformational leadership on display. As Mark has seen what John has seen, experienced what John has experienced and learned what John has learned, Mark has grown as a leader, influencer, and communicator. The information Mark has received, along with the wisdom for its application, has equipped him to now lead all of John's companies.

As a leader, you need to understand the information you share with those you follow is essential to equip them to lead in your absence in the future. The knowledge, experience, insight, and wisdom you impart into the lives of those you are leading, mentoring and training prepares them for the journey they will one day take without you, as they take their turn leading others.

The equipping process informs those you are leading what to do, who do to it with, how to do it, when to do it, where to do it and the all-important why you do it. The transfer of knowledge, insight, experience, and wisdom becomes the catalyst for transformational change in the lives of those you are leading, and the lives of those they will influence in the future.

3. Equipping Prepares

In the movie, *Rocky*, Sylvester Stallone is given the unlikely opportunity to fight the world champion, Apollo Creed, for the heavyweight title. In this real-to-life underdog story, Rocky turns to Mickey, his trainer, to prepare him for the fight. The methods are (at times) unorthodox, such as punching sides of beef in a freezer. But it was the process of equipping Rocky for that fateful fight that prepared him to stand toe-to-toe with the world champion round after round.

While working in the commercial lighting industry in my early 20s, the company I worked with was successful in winning a contract to help re-light Barnhill Arena at the University of Arkansas the last few years that basketball was played there.

While onsite, examining the installation process, I was privileged to watch Nolan Richardson run a basketball practice with his players. The workout was brutal. Running line drills while tossing a weighted ball, shooting free throws at an undersized rim, running plays up and down the court, again and again, the level of intensity never diminished the entire time they were on the court.

At the end of the workout, as these guys gathered around their coach, I overheard Coach Richardson tell his players they were going to be better than the competition as they were going to be better prepared than the competition. The mental, physical and emotional equipping he put these players through again and again toughened them and prepared them to outrun, outlast, out jump and outshoot the competition.

Preparation equips you and your Team members for success. Look at any successful athlete (Michael Jordan, LeBron James, Tiger Woods, Tom Brady, Michael Phelps, and Lindsey Vaughn to name a few) and one thing they all have in common is a commitment to preparation.

The failure to prepare has consequences as well. I was asked to attend the black belt test for a friend of my daughter's a few years back. There were a handful of students testing for their first-degree black belt, and I sat with several of my family members in the spectator section of the school. The forms segment was good, as was their point sparring. I expected this from a school that focused on tournament competition.

But I was aghast when the instructor informed the students they would have to successfully demonstrate self-defense techniques to pass their exam, only to hear the students tell their instructor he had never taught them self-defense techniques at any time during their training. As I watched these young teens fumble and stumble their way through this testing element, I was embarrassed for the students and their parents, angry at the instructor and shocked to see what was being demonstrated as self-defense had little chance of being successful in a real-world fighting scenario.

This instructor failed to equip his students to see success in a key element of martial arts training, the ability to defend oneself. This failure to prepare was obvious, and a glaring gap in the school's curriculum. As a leader, he missed this important equipping element, leaving his students lacking in a key component of martial arts training.

Leaders understand that winning requires preparation. Without preparation, there can be no victory. As a leader, if you don't prepare your team, there can be no success. If the members of a team cannot perform the tasks necessary to reach a stated goal or objective, you have failed as a leader. As a speaker, trainer, and coach, much of my time today is spent helping leaders and future leaders prepare themselves and learn how to pass on what they have learned, so they can equip those on their Team for success.

4. Equipping Multiplies Exponentially

As I previously shared, in first century Jerusalem a charismatic rabbi named Jesus of Nazareth rose to prominence. Unconventional in speech and action, this teacher hand-picked 12 men whom he personally mentored for 3-1/2 years as he traveled the countryside, teaching his message of love and forgiveness to the masses. He was intentional in his equipping of these fishermen, tax collectors and other outcasts from society.

These men continued the teachings of Jesus, their Master Instructor, and this ragtag small group of misfit believers grew to 120, then 3000, then tens of thousands as their teaching spread across the surrounding regions. They continued to meet in homes, synagogues, public squares, and farms. Despite persecution and ridicule, these believers trained and equipped others to also go, teach and make more disciples. The message spread across the known world and by the end of the 20th century, over 2 Billion people around the globe claim to be followers of Christianity.

That's the multiplication power of equipping.

Equipping one person to influence another compounds the opportunity. Two can then become four, exponentially multiplying the ability to influence and change lives. The story of Jesus is but one example of an influential leader who empowered and equipped others to replicate his efforts, which brought about a global movement that continues today.

A negative example of this can be found in examining the rise of Adolph Hitler. Another charismatic leader who began to use his influence to move the masses to follow him to build what he proclaimed would be a thousand-year reign of the German

Empire over the rest of the world. By equipping his followers with a deluded vision of a world that could be, millions of Germans willingly supported this would be Napoleon's rise to power and the subsequent global war that followed.

In the martial arts world, as in life, one person has only so much capacity. At the United States Martial Arts Hall of Fame, each year we honor worthy men and women who have given decades of their life to teach the martial arts. Many of these are solo instructors, teaching in a small setting, for little or no pay, after working an 8 to 5 job somewhere else. They teach and train for the love of the martial arts.

> "Equipping one to influence another compounds the opportunity..."
>
> John Terry

While their years of service are to be commended, what could their legacy have become if they could replicate their efforts in the lives of students? What if they were able to raise others up through the ranks to help carry the load, expand the class size, and influence even more lives with the martial arts?

Equipping does multiply results.

Effective leaders understand the power of equipping and seek every opportunity to teach and train those they are leading. The result is a better version of those who are on the journey, which lends itself to a better outcome for all involved. Equipped followers become the next generation of leaders who are willing to climb the mountain of success alongside the one who knows more and goes before.

Ineffective leaders can't lead indefinitely. Ineffective leaders will not be able to attract and retain the type of talent that makes the team successful for the long-term. An ineffective leader at best can expect mediocre results, and those talented leaders in the making who can take the team to the next level will not follow an ineffective or inept leader for long.

Black belt leaders in life equip those they are leading, so together they can achieve exceptional results.

SUMMARY – Level Seven (Level 1 Brown Belt)

"We must open the doors of opportunity. But we must also equip our people to walk through these doors."
Lyndon B. Johnson

1. Equipping inspires
2. Equipping informs
3. Equipping prepares
4. Equipping multiples exponentially

The Lasting Impact of Loyalty
Chapter Nine

Loyalty has its roots in the character trait of integrity. In the quest of the pursuit of excellence as a Black Belt Leader in Life, the oath of loyalty is a quintessential element for trust. Throughout ancient history, we see men pledge their loyalty to king and country, a cause or a calling, and were willing to sacrifice their very lives to defend it.

By definition, loyalty is a strong feeling of support or allegiance. It is further defined as being firm and consistent in your support or allegiance for someone or something.

In ancient Japan, Samurai would pledge their loyalty in support of their Shogun, dedicating their very lives to protect their leader, his family, and his land. That same pledge of loyalty can be evidenced as you study the exploits of Navy Seals, Army Rangers or other elite tactical units whose code of conduct is a selfless commitment to an ideal, a calling, a mission or a cause.

Many of us saw loyalty on display when the American Embassy was attacked in Benghazi. A handful of highly skilled military personnel came to the defense of the U.S. Ambassador and, though facing superior numbers and armament, valiantly fought to protect the Embassy from hostile forces seeking to wreak havoc on this American installation.

One of the hallmarks of traditional martial arts training today is loyalty to the traditional lineage and history of the Art. The donning of the Gi, the colored belting system, and learning proper etiquette, traditional stances, technique, and movement patterns all are done with an eye on the past, showing loyalty to the tradition of teaching as passed down from instructor to student for hundreds of years.

In religious circles, loyalty plays an essential part in the practice of one's faith. All the major religions of the world share this common thread of loyalty to their founder, and to the adherence to its principles and precepts in the course of daily life. Men have fought and died to defend their religious beliefs throughout history, a tangible demonstration of their loyalty to a cause to which they have pledged their very lives.

Even in geopolitical circles, the character trait of loyalty to a leader or a cause has shaped society and given rise to empires over the years. For years, the sun never set on the British Empire as soldiers and explorers, in loyal obedience to the King (or Queen), sought to colonize much of the known world. The rise and fall of the Nazi Empire during WW2 is a testament to how loyalty to a leader or a cause can be taken to an extreme, resulting in the death of millions of innocents in a senseless global war for domination of the world.

Loyalty to a nation remains a hallmark of citizenship. A few years ago, I was invited to be a special guest of honor for an international martial arts tournament held on the beautiful Caribbean island of St. Lucia. Competitors from other Caribbean islands, South America and Europe were in attendance. The level of competition was intense, as the competitors were not only competing for individual awards; they were representing their country at this tournament.

In marketing, creating brand loyalty is paramount to lasting success. Billions of dollars are spent annually by corporate America (and global corporations as well) to build and maintain a loyal following. Think about coffee and who first comes to mind? For millions of Americans, it's Starbucks.

Starbucks has mastered the art of gaining "loyalty" among its followers. They understand that loyalty builds trust, and trust builds repeat business, and repeat business means lasting success.

Apparel companies like Nike, Under Armor, and Adidas also understand this. Technology companies like Apple, Samsung, AT&T, and Verizon do too. Franchises like McDonald's, Taco Bell, Burger King or Chic-fil-A are also masters of "brand loyalty". And don't forget retail giants like Amazon, Wal-Mart and Kroger have their own loyal following as well.

In leadership, loyalty is essential. Without loyalty, there can be no trust. Without trust, followers will not follow a leader for very long. Consider Apple. Steve Jobs bucked the mainstream to create a platform that was different, innovative, simple to use and reliable. That fostered trust in those who followed. Today, when Apple announces a new iPhone, people will line up days in advance to acquire the "latest and greatest" from a company that has built an incredible fan base of loyal followers.

If we are going to lead people, and have the opportunity to influence them for a long time, then we have to embrace loyalty as an essential character trait we live out and model for others. That means we have to be men or women of integrity, as this is where loyalty is derived.

Loyalty in a leader is manifested in four key areas:

1. Loyalty to yourself.

My parents valued integrity and loyalty as chief among the character traits they wanted to see cultivated in the lives of their children. One of my Mom's constant reminders to me was, *"John, be true to yourself."* Integrity, loyal and fidelity were the benchmarks by which my parents taught me to live my life, and the example which they lived before me.

In a prior chapter, I shared the story of Mahatma Gandhi, who would not ask a young boy to quit eating sugar until he was sugar-free himself. Gandhi knew he would not be true to himself if he asked the young boy to sacrifice what he was unwilling to give up. This is a visual example of being loyal to oneself.

Visit any Gym or Fitness Center in January and you'll see people signing up to get in shape, lose weight or improve their overall health. Late December and early January are perhaps the best months for gym membership enrollment annually. Why? We've been conditioned that we make "New Year's Resolutions" to start afresh and anew, and a plethora of TV, radio and social media ads make sure we are reminded of this conditioned response.

Loyalty to oneself can be seen in February, March, April and the remainder of the year when those who are *"true to themselves"* are still in the gym at least 3 times a week, diligently working to reach (or surpass) their initial fitness goal. The dedication to renewing that membership, and keep working on oneself, is a testimony to a person who is truly being true to themselves.

Loyalty to yourself means you actually do the work required in order to reach a goal, complete a task or accomplish an objective. My business partner and I made it a point in our martial arts schools that we would do the workout alongside our students, as we didn't want to ask our students to do what we were unwilling to do ourselves. Nor did we want to be the stereotypical martial arts instructor or athletic coach who was overweight, out of shape and could no longer effectively "do" the martial arts.

Being loyal to oneself requires discipline. If you intend to be a Black Belt Leader in Life, it is essential. The secret to your success, according to John Maxwell, is found in your daily routine. You can't reach your potential without sacrifice, and loyalty to oneself is that commitment to do daily what is required to put yourself in a position to achieve success and significance. It is you doing those things daily (by default) you would ask others to do if they were a part of your Team. Loyalty is being true to YOU!

It is the height of hypocrisy to ask others to do what you are unwilling to do yourself. Leaders GO BEFORE and as such lead by example. The character traits, values and beliefs you expect to see in others you should first emulate in your own life. It means that you're willing to roll up your sleeves and get dirty right alongside your Team members if that is what it takes to get the job done.

How can you successfully lead people where you haven't gone? The wagon trains that took settlers across the breadth of America were led by seasoned guides who knew the topography and what was required to safely navigate the journey. They knew what they were capable of, were honest about the risks that lay ahead, and didn't ask those on the journey with them to take risks they were unwilling to take on their own.

Loyalty to yourself means being true to yourself. It means the very character traits, values, and beliefs you expect to see cultivated in your followers have first been cultivated in you. It also means understanding your own strengths, and your weaknesses, and developing your unique skill set accordingly.

Loyalty to yourself is about living a life of integrity. As my Grandma used to tell me, *"It means your saying and your doing look and act the same, all the time."* You cannot expect loyalty from others if you cannot be honest with yourself, and live a life of integrity and consistency that will inspire others to trust and follow you.

Being loyal to yourself manifests itself in your daily habit. Successful people do daily what unsuccessful people are not willing to do. Being consistent in temperament, attitude and action are hallmarks of a person who is loyal to themselves - and can expect loyalty from others.

2. Loyalty to your family.

I grew up in a home that valued loyalty. My father was a lay minister and he was a man who was consistent in word and deed. He was my first mentor, my first coach, and my first trainer. My mom, a housewife, was committed to my dad and lived a life of devotion and loyalty to her husband and her children.

My sister and I witnessed this powerful bond of loyalty. My beliefs were strongly influenced by the consistent example my parents displayed as they were loyal to themselves and to each other. That bond of loyalty and commitment meant that we could trust each other to honor our word and that we were dedicated to the welfare and well-being of one another in our family.

Family loyalty can manifest itself in other areas as well. In the martial arts community, your instructor and training partners

> "The foundation stones for a balanced success are honesty, character, integrity, faith, love and loyalty..."
>
> Zig Ziglar

often become your "brothers and sisters" in the Art. Loyalty to those in your school is earned as you train together, learn together, build rapport, and push each other to truly discover what you're capable of doing, as you pursue your next rank advancement.

At the United States Martial Arts Hall of Fame, we gather once a year for a celebration of the global martial arts community. This event opens with a 3-day training camp, featuring a different instructor teaching a different discipline each hour. There is an appreciation for each style or system represented, and an openness and willingness to learn from each other. Why? We are part of a global family of martial arts practitioners who are continuing the traditions of those who came before. It's family sharing with family. Loyalty in action.

You also see this in the Armed forces and law enforcement community. As you train daily with your fellow soldiers or officers, you build a rapport that causes you to "become one" with those in your squad or platoon. In conflict, that level of loyalty causes men and women to band together, even when facing overwhelming odds, to fight, and to sacrifice themselves, for those alongside them.

When I am traveling, and in need, I know I can call on one of my martial arts brothers and sisters and they will do what they can to help. That same loyalty to family is seen in motorcycle clubs, as well as in law enforcement and military circles. It's family taking care of family, loyalty in action.

Sadly, our nation saw this same loyalty to family in the rise of organized crime around the turn of the 20th century, as crime "families" were established and gained a foothold in American society. The rank and file members of each Mafia family pledged their lives and loyalty to the crime boss, a father-figure. Today, we see this same twisted "family loyalty" in many of the gangs that are now commonplace in major cities across the United States, and in other parts of the world. These individuals will live and die, steal and kill, for the sake of "family".

3. Loyalty to your calling.

Your calling is what defines you in your role as a leader. It sets you apart and distinguishes you as unique among others; it is the practical fulfillment of your passionate dream. Your calling is what you were put on this earth to do, and how you're making a difference in some way, for some cause, that beckons to others to join you on your quest.

Nelson Mandela saw the oppression of black Africans in South Africa during a time of segregation known as Apartheid. He was only one man, but he was committed to speaking out against the injustice being inflicted on his people. Though he was imprisoned for his efforts, this passion to make a difference, to right a wrong, continued to burn brightly. His loyalty to seeing a change in the culture of his country inspired others to join him on this journey for equality and put an end to this discriminatory practice.

America went through a similar chapter in our nation. Though the actions of President Lincoln freed the slaves, equality was not achieved for many years to follow. A young, black minister by the name of Martin Luther King Jr. began to speak about not being judged by the color of one's skin, but the content of one's heart. His non-violent approach to bridging the racial divide rallied millions to his cause and ushered in a new era that ended segregation in America.

What if Nelson Mandela or Dr. King had not been loyal to their calling? What if they had given up on being a catalyst for change when they were persecuted, afflicted, or jailed? If, before their followers, they betrayed their trust by turning their backs on the very issue they were trying to address, the wrong they were trying to right, what would have been their future? Would the masses have joined the cause if the one leading the cause was not loyal to staying the course?

In ancient Japan, the Samurai held to a strict code of conduct. They were tasked with the protection of their overlord, the Shogun. This was their passion, their calling, and their entire lives were lived in preparation to assume this role as defender and protector of their Master, his family, and his land. The Clan of the Samurai lived as one, in a strict hierarchical order. If a Samurai betrayed his calling, he was excommunicated from the Clan and became known as a Ronin, a Samurai without a Master.

Nothing negatively affects a leader more than disloyalty to his or her calling. To turn your back on your passion, your calling, is to betray the trust and confidence of those who are following. When a leader is no longer loyal to his or her calling, their opportunity to influence and be a positive change agent is significantly diminished, if not altogether lost.

4. Loyalty to your Team.

The vast majority of men and women who don the blue uniform of law enforcement do so because, to them, this is a calling. They are passionate about protecting and serving their community. It takes a special person to don the uniform each day, say goodbye to their wife and children, not knowing if they are coming back at the end of their shift.

I had the privilege of being one of the very first Boy Scout Police Explorers in my hometown as a teenager, giving me an inside look at the world of law enforcement, and it profoundly impacted my life. My respect for these men and women was (and is) so strong, I later volunteered to serve as a law enforcement and emergency services chaplain for a season.

I watched and often rode alongside these public servants as they responded to auto accidents, fires, drownings, thefts, domestic violence, drunk driving, and more. These men and women routinely experience the worst that life has to offer, and they are there to bring hope to the hopeless, help to the helpless and even in their interactions with those who were on the wrong side of the law, they treated offenders with dignity and respect.

One night, an officer was injured as he worked a traffic stop. His car was rear-ended by a drunk driver, crushing the officer's legs. When the call went out, city, county and state law enforcement rushed to the aid of a fellow officer who was down. They came alongside his family as he recovered, as he was a fellow brother in blue. They supported him and his family until he was back on his feet, and back to work.

Recently, a martial arts instructor, who is also a law enforcement officer, was riding his Harley to Oklahoma City to attend the United States Martial Arts Hall of Fame. He lost control of his bike on loose gravel and went down. He rolled several times before coming to a stop on the side of the Interstate. The bike was totaled. It was a bad wreck.

As he looked up, in severe pain, he saw his foot was pointing the wrong direction. His femur was broken, as was his wrist and hand. He was bruised and bloodied and in need of immediate care. A state trooper arrived on the scene, and once he learned this was a fellow officer, he radioed for an air ambulance, telling the dispatcher "one of our brothers is down."

The officers not only rushed him to the hospital, but they also followed up to make sure he was okay, demonstrating the powerful bond that exists among members of the law enforcement community. Fellow officers from his own department came to the aid of him and his wife, collecting his broken motorcycle and trailering it home, and continue to follow up as this officer continues to make a full recovery.

Loyalty to your team means that you give them your very best, not your leftovers. It means honoring your word, following through with your commitments and giving them what they need in order to see success. It means giving them strong, consistent support, along with your allegiance, to the cause or outcome you're seeking to achieve together.

Without loyalty, a Team cannot see significant achievement in any cause or action they put their hands to do. Without loyalty, there is no trust. Where there is no trust, motives are questioned and everyone cares more about their own self-interests than the accomplishments of the Team.

Without loyalty, a Team cannot remain cohesive when problems or challenges arise. Teams that lack loyalty become disjointed, uncooperative and eventually disband. Without the bonds of loyalty holding the individual members of a Team together, the likelihood that anything of lasting value will be achieved is significantly diminished.

Zig Ziglar said, "*The foundation stones for a balanced success are honesty, character, integrity, faith, love, and loyalty.*" Loyalty embodies the character traits of honesty, integrity, faith, and love - to yourself, your family, your calling and your Team. Loyalty is an essential trait for anyone who wants to be a Black Belt Leader in Life.

SUMMARY – Level Eight (Level 2 Brown Belt)

"Soldiers, when committed to a task, can't compromise. Its unrelenting devotion to the standards of duty and courage, absolute loyalty to others, not letting the task go until it's done."

John Keegan

1. Loyalty to yourself.
2. Loyalty to your family.
3. Loyalty to your calling.
4. Loyalty to your Team.

The Power of Transformation
Chapter Ten

My core martial arts system is Shobayashi Shorin-Ryu. Its founder was Eizo Shimabukuro, who passed away in 2017. His lineage includes Anko Itosu (considered by many to be the founder of modern Karate), along with influential Karate pioneers Chotoku Kyan, Chosin Chibana and Chojun Miyagi.

The Chinese martial arts made their way to Okinawa in the 14th Century, but really become prominent in the 18th Century when Kusanku, a Chinese military official, began doing demonstrations and teaching Chinese arts to island natives. As the indigenous Okinawan martial arts were later blended with the Chinese by several practitioners of the Arts, the fighting styles combined to become what today is known as Karate.

Gichin Funakoshi (founder of Shotokan) took Karate to Japan, where it was codified in the country's educational system. A colored belt system was added, and from there Karate has spread to nearly every part of the known world today. It is one of the most prolific arts taught globally today.

Karate has had a transformational impact on the global martial arts community. Soldiers stationed in Okinawa during and after World War II had the opportunity to train with these pioneers of the martial arts and brought Karate to America. Nearly every major city in the United States today has at least one Karate school perpetuating the Art and continuing the legacy of Itosu.

The martial arts are transformative. Students who enroll get physically stronger. Their minds become more alert, and they exude an air of quiet confidence, knowing they are prepared to respond in the event of trouble. This was especially true of our female students, who learned to face their fears and discover they were able to live life without being afraid. Many of the adults who joined our program saw their bodies firm up, as they burned off excess body fat and their muscles toned and hardened from the workouts. Stamina and endurance increased as well.

For younger students, focus improved. Grades in school also saw improvement. Their level of respect and courtesy displayed toward their parents and others improved as well. They were less likely to be bullied at school. Children with learning disabilities (such as Asperger's or mild [high functioning] autism) became more coordinated, interacted better with others, and often saw improved academic scores as well.

The power of transformation is amazing. One lady who took one of our women's self-defense classes was blind. As she began to learn what it meant to live life situationally aware, and how she could use some simple, but effective, techniques to deal with an attacker, "Mom" (as we all affectionately called her) was no longer timid when she walked out on the floor.

About week four or five of our 12-week program, "Mom" owned the floor when she came to class. When one of our instructors would engage in a simulated attack, they were met with a ferocity that was fun to watch – unless you were on the receiving end. She would grab her attacker, and not let go as she beat the daylights out of them.

I failed to mention that "Mom" was a retired Masseuse (massage therapist), and had a grip of steel. When she grabbed one of our attackers, it was like being in the grip of an anaconda. She would not let go until the attacker was immobilized on the ground. *"I see with my hands,"* she would say, *"and once I can see you, I'm not letting go!"* Many a night all our instructors went home bloodied and bruised; a testament to the power of transformation in the life of a disabled woman who learned to defend herself.

As a leader, the highest calling on your life is to become a transformational leader. In *The 5 Levels of Leadership*, John Maxwell outlines five stages of leadership development:

- Position – Lead from a Position
- Permission – Lead others with their Permission
- Production – Lead others to become Productive
- People Development – Developing other leaders
- Pinnacle – Legacy leadership building

If you've incorporated and internalized the other character traits along your leadership journey, you're now about to enter the next phase of your Black Belt Leadership training – TRANSFORMATION!

Transformation, by definition, is a metamorphosis or marked change that takes place in the life of a person who has gone through a process that has refined or altered them in some way. We see this physically as we watch a tiny baby grow to adulthood, or an acorn reaches to the sky as it transforms to become a massive oak tree. Transformation, by definition, means to change.

Transformation is a powerful process that is life-altering and can put you in a position to achieve success and live a life of significance. It prepares you to help others go through the process of transforming themselves and can ultimately leave a leadership legacy to future generations.

Transformation is change, and it begins within.

1. Transformation changes you.

As a Black Belt Leader in Life, you begin to experience transformation as you start to take responsibility for your own personal growth and development. You invest time and resources into yourself so you can become a better version of you. As you begin to incorporate the character traits taught in this book into your daily routine, you begin to change how you think, act, speak and feel as you grow and mature as a leader.

You cannot take others where you have not gone yourself. The art of transformation is the process of taking yourself on a personal journey of growth and maturity, so you can prepare yourself to take others on a similar journey in the future. Before you can inspire others to change, you must change yourself to become a better version of YOU!

The historical narrative of Moses is an interesting study in the power of transformation. He was born at a time when the Israelites lived in Egypt when a decree had gone out from Pharaoh to kill all the male Hebrew children as a means of population control. Moses' mother built a small basket to hide her child among the reeds of the river, where he was discovered and adopted by the Pharaoh's own daughter.

Having been raised as a son of Egypt throughout his formative years, Moses rejected his adoptive Egyptian lineage when he saw a guard abusing an Israeli slave and murders him. He fled to the desert where he became a desert sheepherder for the next 40 years.

According to ancient writings, Moses had an encounter with God at a burning bush, where he was called to return to Egypt to deliver the Israelites from enslavement. We see in the text Moses transformed from a fearful sheepherder who stutters to a fearless leader who boldly stands up to Pharaoh, demanding (and ultimately securing) the release of the Israelites.

Before Moses could lead others, he had to learn to lead himself. Forty years as a sheepherder was his transformational academy. Sheep can be stubborn, and at times really stupid. They are ill-equipped to defend themselves and rely on the shepherd to lead them from pasture to pasture and brook to brook. His "burning bush" moment was graduation day when it was time to face his fear and become the leader he was destined to become.

Arnold Schwarzenegger's parents had other plans for him as a youth, but he wanted to be a bodybuilder. His dad wanted him to follow in his steps as a police officer and his mother wanted him to go to a trade school upon graduation. He became obsessed with bodybuilding and began a workout regimen to become the next Steve Reeves or Johnny Weissmuller.

Schwarzenegger went on to win the Mr. Universe title at the age of 20 and won the Mr. Olympia title seven times. From there, he mounted a very successful film and political career, transforming himself time and again to meet the challenges that lay ahead.

Students entering our dojo were often quick to ask how long it would take to earn their black belt. Our response to them was that the black belt wasn't the end of the journey, but the next chapter. As they began to transform their thinking from a destination (earning a black belt) to a journey (learning to live as a black belt leader in life), how they trained changed, as did how they lived their lives both in and out of the dojo.

Leadership is no different. Whether by position or permission, when we are given the privilege of leading, it demands something of ourselves. Unless we have gone through the transformation process (or at least started down this path), our ability to lead ourselves and others effectively will be limited, at best.

Pastor Rick Warren, author of the *Purpose Driven Life* said, *"Transformation is a process, and as life happens there are tons of ups and downs. It's a journey of discovery – there are moments on mountaintops and moments in deep valleys of despair."*

It is when we begin to transform ourselves, to change from within. We give ourselves permission to become a better version of ourselves than we are today. As we invest in our own personal growth and development, we have the privilege to become a personal agent for positive change in our own lives – which then serves as an inspiration for others.

2. Transformation changes those around you.

The process of personal transformation is contagious. Like an inspirational virus, it spreads to those around you, infecting them with the passion and desire to change themselves.

In the 1960 movie classic, *Spartacus*, there is an epic scene when the Roman soldiers surround and confront a group of surviving rebels as they search for the gladiator-leader of the rebellion Spartacus. When the corrupt Roman senator, Crassus, offers a pardon (and a return to slavery) if the slave army will turn over their leader, one by one these men respond, "*I am Spartacus!*"

Spartacus was a slave who saw the corruption of Rome and wanted to free his people from enslavement. He was sentenced to death by starvation only to be discovered as a ferocious fighter. He was later sold to a gladiatorial school where he was trained as a gladiator, and later (along with his fellow gladiators) overthrew his captors and escaped into the Italian countryside.

> "Transformation is a process...It's a journey of discovery..."
>
> Rick Warren

As Spartacus transformed himself, he became an influential leader who fought for a cause greater than himself. His example inspired others to pick up their swords and follow this dynamic leader who again and again defeats multiple armies before being surrounded by overwhelming forces at the conclusion of the movie.

Rather than give up their beloved leader, these men became the embodiment of their leader, one who was willing to sacrifice his life for the freedom of his people. These slave army soldiers choose death by crucifixion over betraying their leader because they saw in Spartacus' leadership example the embodiment of the freedom they longed for.

John Wesley was a passionate, charismatic 18th-century cleric. After what he defines as an evangelical (transformational) calling, he began to traverse Great Britain and Ireland, preaching outdoors. It has been said that Wesley would go to a particular field and begin to preach, even if no one was present. As his fame and popularity grew, people would come to hear Wesley preach then ask where he would be the next day. Crowds began to swell as he traveled from place to place, later establishing churches across the land.

One particular story tells of the time when Wesley was approached by a newspaper reporter who had heard of the growing popularity of this itinerant preacher and asked how he was able to attract such a large audience to hear him speak.

By some accounts, John Wesley replied, "*I simply set myself on fire, and people come to watch me burn.*" Wesley went on to found Methodism and became known as one of the most beloved men in all of England before his death. Wesley's inspirational teaching inspired the birth of a denomination that today still has a global impact, a testament to the fact that transformation not only changes the person, it changes others as well.

3. Transformation enlarges your dream

I had the privilege of meeting Maria Conceicao in February 2018, and to hear her amazing story of personal transformation. Maria was working as a flight attendant when she had a 24-hour layover in Dhaka, Bangladesh (a country of 19 million). It was the first time she witnessed poverty on such a large scale. She was so moved by the experience, she wanted to make a difference.

In 2005, she sold all her belongings, cashed in her bank accounts, asked her friend to donate whatever they had they did not need, and she returned to Bangladesh to make a difference.

Committed to making a difference, and lacking in funds, she began to search for ways to raise money. A series of Internet searches has led her to pursue what some would call an "outlandish dream" to raise money for people in a land that was not her own.

Conceicao's fundraising efforts have included summiting Mt. Kilimanjaro in Africa in 2010 and completed a successful trek to the North Pole and walking a marathon on each of the 7 emirates in the United Arab Emirates in 2011. In 2013, she became the first Portuguese woman to summit Mt. Everest and has since run seven ultra-marathons on seven continents in six weeks, seven ultra-marathons in seven days, and seven marathons on seven continents in eleven days.

Maria holds 6 Guinness World Records and recently fell short in her efforts to swim the English Channel due to bad weather. This from a girl who was not an athlete, had no formal training, and could not swim. Maria's transformation as a compassionate difference maker in Bangladesh continues to enlarge her vision of what can be done – and demonstrates the influential power a single life can have as a global difference maker.

At the end of hearing Maria's story, the audience of 2000 plus spontaneously responded and for the next 15 minutes, people walked to the stage, dropping money as they passed by. As staff scrambled to find containers to hold the money, people continued to come forward. Wave after wave, it continued. I have never witnessed anything like this in my life.

By the time the giving concluded, $140,000 was given to support the Maria Christina Foundation's ongoing efforts to better the lives of the people of Bangladesh. Maria is not done, she still has BIG DREAMS, but as a transformational leader, she knows that she can inspire others to join her on this quest to make a difference in the lives of a people group who can never give anything back but a thank you.

The dreams of a transformational leader are contagious, and as you continue to grow and expand in your leadership ability, your dream will grow and expand as well.

4. Transformation creates a legacy

A transformational leader inspires others. Dale Carnegie was an American author and lecturer who specialized in writing and course creation in the areas of self-development, public speaking, communication, and sales. In 1936, he authored, *How to Win Friends and Influence People* – which was an immediate bestseller and remains popular (and relevant) even today.

While an unemployed actor living in the local YMCA, Carnegie wanted to teach public speaking. He convinced the YMCA to host the event, and it was there he perfected the techniques to help his students overcome their fear of public speaking.

Carnegie was passionate about helping others become skilled in the art of public speaking, as well as how to become an effective communicator and influencer of others. It is said he critiqued over 150,000 speeches during his lifetime and went on to inspire millions to become better speakers, communicators, and influencers, both in business and in life.

Dale Carnegie died in 1955, yet his legacy continues. Beyond the grave, Carnegie continues to mold, shape, and influence countless lives because he became a transformational leader.

In *The 5 Levels of Leadership"*, John Maxwell teaches the Pinnacle (Level 5) is the ultimate goal of a leader. Few will ever get there, but for those who do, the influence they make on the world, and the legacy they leave behind, is tremendous. A Level 5 leader is one who builds legs to his or her legacy by raising up leaders who are not only transformational leaders but develop others along the way to also become leaders themselves.

Legacy leaders are reproducers. They build an organization that will live beyond their years. Sam Walton is an example of a legacy leader. From humble beginnings in Bentonville AR with the Walton Five and Dime to a global empire that is the Wal-Mart and Sam's Club brand, Walton built an organization around an idea that today reaches into more than 15 international markets.

Another legacy leader is General William Booth, founder of the Salvation Army in 1865. With an initial focus of "Soup, Soap, and Salvation" Booth and his wife Catherine began to envision an organization that could help those trapped in the woes of alcoholism, drug addiction, prostitution, and other moral vices, as well as the poor and destitute, to find hope and a future.

Today, the organization boasts more than 1.7 million members worldwide, operating in over 130 countries around the globe. The Salvation Army runs charity shops, homeless shelters, and provides disaster relief and humanitarian aid to developing countries among its other good works.

I was privileged in July 2018 to spend a few hours with Mike Dillard, the founder of Century Martial Arts. Century is the largest manufacturer of martial arts equipment and supplies in the world. My daughter, Jessie, was with me. As Mike took us on a tour of one of his plants, we were amazed at the enormity of their operation, and to see the humble beginnings of what is now truly a martial arts supply empire. To see the equipment they designed, to build equipment that had never before existed, was a testament to the innovation and creative spirit that flourishes at Century.

Mike's humbleness impressed me. It was hot and humid in Oklahoma City the day we visited, and there was an issue with air conditioning in parts of the plant. Before we started our tour, Mike stopped in to see the H/R department to make sure fans were being distributed, additional water was made available, and that the employees were given additional breaks during the day to get a respite from the heat.

As we met the Team members and talked about the future of the global martial arts community, it was apparent that Mike Dillard is a transformational, Level 5 leader who is developing the leaders around him and building an organization that will be a lasting monument and legacy to a true innovator in the martial arts supply business. He and his Team continues to innovate, continues to dream, continues to ask, "What's next?" as they continue to transform the martial arts supply landscape.

As a leader transforms first within and then transforms those around them, the dream and vision of "what can be" enlarges within. The transformational leader moves beyond what is possible to begin to believe and envision the impossible.

- How far can we go?
- How many lives can we change?
- What lasting impact can we make?
- What's next as we continue to move ahead?

These are the thoughts of a transformational leader. To be a Black Belt Leader in Life is to be a transformational change agent.

I wonder how many martial arts school owners today (or any business owner for that matter) are giving consideration not only to how they make a difference in what they do today, but who they are investing in, who they are growing and maturing who will take their place tomorrow? What will be their legacy when they are gone?

Transformation is change. It starts within, and then reaches out to change the lives of others. Transformation enlarges the dream of the dreamer, as well as their capacity to achieve the impossible as they develop the leaders around them to leave a lasting legacy.

SUMMARY – Level Nine (Level 3 Brown Belt)

"Yes, your transformation will be hard. Yes, you will feel frightened, messed up and knocked down. Yes, you'll want to stop. Yes, it's the best work you'll ever do."

Robin Sharma

1. Transformation changes you.
2. Transformation changes those around you.
3. Transformation enlarges your dream.
4. Transformation creates a legacy.

Living Life as a Black Belt Leader in Life
Chapter Eleven

Our school, like many martial arts schools, offered a Beginner's Program for young children. Ours was a "skills and drills" focused program adapted from the Century Lil Dragons™ curriculum, coupled with a values-based emphasis to reinforce things like discipline, respect, truthfulness, cooperation and integrity in these young minds. Children as young as four learned to punch, kick and block. They also learned the importance of honoring and respecting their parents, their peers, and how to work together.

We had fun in our class. LOTS of fun! Laughter and encouragement were hallmarks of our teaching model.

However, even with all the laughter and the fun, it was not uncommon for children to be a bit hesitant the first time they visited our school. One of the first things we taught new students was basic blocking techniques. We would play a game with a blocking pad, "*Whack a Dragon*" (as they called it), where we would try to touch a pad on the child's head before he or she could raise their arm and block the pad.

The first few times we would attempt to touch the pad to a child's head, their arm would rise after we'd tapped them on the head. Parents would laugh as their child's arm slowly rose above their head, pushing the pad up and off their noggin. We would repeat the process, as they stood in a circle, not knowing who was going to be targeted next with the blocking pad.

Once they got the hang of the game, it was difficult, if not impossible, to touch the pad to their head before they blocked it. The new students gained confidence they could learn martial arts, in a safe and fun environment, and the parents were pleased to see their children learning and having fun. The fact we are also reinforcing important character values was a plus and proved to be one of the "sticky factors" in keeping kids enrolled.

After a few weeks in our program, these young students would spontaneously block when a punch, a kick or a blocking pad was directed at them. Without thinking, their arms would rise, swing outward, swing down or move to either block or redirect the punch or kick. It was an "A-ha" moment for students and parents alike, as they were internalizing the important safety skills that were an integral part of learning the martial arts for self-defense and confidence.

We would then add an age-appropriate countermeasure to what the children were learning, and in a few weeks, this too became an automatic response. When confronted with various self-defense scenarios, the students had conditioned their bodies to "act without thinking", triggering an automated response to protect themselves from an aggressor.

"Acting without thinking" is the essence of martial arts training. In fact, any combative art (including those taught to our military and law enforcement), is essentially what I like to refer to as "Predictable Response Training". In the Orient, it is referred to as "Mushin" (literally, no mind).

Watch any world-class athlete perform, and their bodies simply do the task assigned to them. They don't think; they just do. Watch a veteran law enforcement officer handcuff an assailant or a Special Forces soldier deploy into a combat situation and you see predictable response training (Mushin) in action.

In martial arts, and in life, the concept of Mushin is that you train your mind and your body to respond almost without conscious thought. In the martial arts, and in law enforcement, you learn to read the other person's demeanor, body language, and non-verbal cues, as well as what the person may be saying, to look for tell-tale signs an attack is about to ensue. When a punch or kick is thrown, or an assailant attempts to grab or choke you, you have repeatedly trained your body to anticipate this, and muscle memory takes over, allowing you to perform a countermeasure almost without conscious thought. That's Mushin.

I have had the privilege of training in combat shooting with instructors who train members of the Israeli Defense Forces (IDF). For hours and days, we drill the mechanics...how to draw the weapon, charge the weapon, aim and shoot the weapon, change magazines, deal with misfires, and holster the weapon. It is only after we have honed these skills to muscle memory that we move on to tactical training.

Why is this so important in martial arts? If you're attacked by an aggressor, or multiple aggressors, you don't have time to think, "*Ok, I'm getting attacked, what I do now?*" And you sure don't have time to Google or watch a YouTube video on how to defend yourself from a rear naked choke. You've got about 8-10 seconds before you're unconscious, drooling all over yourself.

If a knife, gun, or other weapon is involved, the threat level is even higher. Adrenaline begins to surge through your body, affecting your emotions, your thinking, your reflexes and more. If you haven't trained your body for an automated response, your chances of a successful outcome significantly diminish.

144

In business, and in life, the concept of Mushin is the same. We practice Mushin in our daily routine. Most of us don't think about our early morning preparation process, we do it automatically. We don't give conscious thought to taking a shower, dressing, eating breakfast, brushing our teeth and driving to work. We become creatures of habit (predictable response training) and we simply do, without really thinking.

How much of what you do at work is Mushin? Do you consciously think about typing on a keyboard, or do you sit down and begin to type? If we will all be honest, we have automated much of our daily routine, at work and at home. We live our lives without thinking, settling for mediocre or average in the process.

To achieve Black Belt level as a leader, you have to become intentional. You can't just live life by default. In order to grow and see your dreams become reality, you have to be intentional. A pack of seeds will not grow until someone is intentional about putting the seeds in the proper environment, watering the soil, adding nutrients and providing sunlight for the seed to grow.

It is the same way with our lives as leaders. If you want to be a Black Belt Leader in Life at home, at work, in your church or your community, you have to be intentional. You have to have a growth plan that you follow, training yourself to become a better version of YOU each and every single day.

I was recently with John Maxwell at the International Maxwell Conference in Orlando. He reminded those of us in the room of one of the steps to being an intentional leader, one who refuses to live life by default. John shared one of his more famous quotes, *"The secret to your success is found in your daily routine."*

One of your challenges, as a leader, is to create your own personal growth plan. As I shared with you in Chapter One, the character traits of a Black Belt Leader in Life have been outlined in this book. This book is a training manual intended to help you create a *"Mushin Mind"* when it comes to being a leader.

How do you do that? You begin to incorporate these character traits of a Black Belt Leader into your daily routine until they become a natural part of who you are. If you will spend 30 days on a single character trait, internalizing it until it becomes a habit. You make it a part of who you are. That trait becomes Mushin, something you do, without conscious thought.

> "The secret to your success is found in your daily routine."
>
> John Maxwell

Being intentional about developing a *"Mushin Mind"* when it comes to leadership may sound like an oxymoron, but it is essential if you want to truly be a Black Belt Leader in Life. So what do I mean by that?

First, you have to believe in yourself. Remember, you cannot ask others to go where you haven't gone before, so you've got to believe in YOU. A positive self-image is essential to believe that you can grow, you can mature, your dreams can be achieved, and you can lead yourself, and others.

You have to believe that leadership is valuable, and there is a need for leadership in your own life, and in the lives of others. You have to believe leadership is your calling, and be willing to pay the cost to become a Black Belt Leadership in Life. John Maxwell says becoming a leader will cost you, sooner than you think, more than you think and more often than you think.

"Nothing can be achieved that you do not believe."
John Terry

Secondly, you have to commit to becoming a lifetime student of learning. A black belt in martial arts is not a sign you've made it, that you've arrived. It is a sign that you're fully committed to a being a serious, lifetime student of the Arts.

Every true Black Belt Leader in Life practices humility and is open and honest with those around him or her. You must understand and embrace the fact that true leadership is a journey, not a destination. It requires you to not only be committed to lead but also following those who are ahead of you on the journey, allowing you to continue to learn and hone your leadership skills.

"A lifetime of learning equips for a lifetime of leading." wow!
John Terry

Next comes accountability. Being a leader is much more than simply having a title or a position. It also means that you are personally responsible for whatever happens. You are responsible for yourself, for those who are mentoring you to grow and improve, and for the journey itself. You're also ultimately responsible for your followers.

Black Belt Leaders in Life don't pass the buck. You can't make excuses as a leader. Good or bad, they both fall squarely on your shoulders. You must take responsibility when things go wrong, and be sure to give the credit to the team when things go right.

"Neither age nor experience matters when it comes to being personally responsible for any and all of my outcomes."
Kory Livingstone

After accountability, you have to become an efficient, effective communicator. Communication takes place only when the speaker and the hearer understand the same information exactly as it was intended to be shared. Is it any wonder that few people really connect when it comes to communicating, as we aren't assuring the message we are conveying is being understood by those we are delivering it to so mutual understanding takes place.

It is not only what you say, but when and how you say it. Clarity of the message is important, as it is easy to complicate even the simplest of messages. The KISS Method (Keep It Sweet and Simple) of communication works well for Black Belt Leaders.

Not only is clarity important, but also consistency. What you say and what you do should align. No one wants to follow a leader who says one thing, yet does another. Hypocrisy is the death knell of a leader, for no one will follow a leader for long whose saying and doing misalign.

> *"Wise men speak because they have something to say.*
> *Fools because they have to say something."*
>
> **Plato**

Black Belt Leaders are kinetic, men and women of action. You can't be passive and expect to be a leader of people. Those who are following you are doing so because they expect you to take decisive action to bring a dream to life, achieve a goal or see a task to completion.

Kinetic leaders internalize what they believe, and demonstrate that daily before those who are following. You must be able to pass on what you've learned to those who are following, equipping and training them to become better, more equipped, versions of themselves.

As a Black Belt Leader, your actions must be consistent with your values and convictions. What is inside you is ultimately manifested on the outside. When there is a misalignment of values, convictions, and actions, trust is eroded. And when you cannot be trusted, few remain committed to following you for long.

One of the more humorous statements I've heard John Maxwell make many times is, *"If you think you're leading, and no one is following, you're only taking a walk."* Action-focused leaders whose values and convictions are lived out in their actions attract like-minded followers.

> **"Do you want to know who you are? Don't ask, ACT!**
> **Action will delineate and define you."**
> **Thomas Jefferson**

Black Belt Leaders are also bold and are willing to attempt the improbable, the impossible. This is a by-product of being kinetic, action-focused. As a leader, you should be moving forward toward the realization of your dream, your goal. You should possess a *"Can Do"* attitude that sees the challenges ahead not as an insurmountable obstacle but as an opportunity to learn, to grow, something that can be overcome.

As a bold leader, you instill and inspire boldness in others. When those who are following see you pressing forward, despite the challenges that lie ahead of you, something rises up within them that says, *"I can do this too."* Now you aren't taking on obstacles and problems alone; those who are following are alongside you, boldly pushing forward with you.

This compounds, literally multiplies, your results. King Solomon of ancient Israel once said, *"Two are better than one, for they have a good reward for their labor. A three-stranded cord is not easily broken."* When your boldness is on display, it is attractional, and as a result, the intellectual, creative, physical and emotional collective of the team is released. Problems are solved, questions are answered, and results are compounded, multiplied.

Boldness is not arrogance. Arrogance takes boldness to a dangerous place, where prudence and caution are thrown out the window and you blindly charge forward without an action plan. Arrogance is thinking too highly of yourself, too little of the challenge that lies ahead, and fails to consider the consequences to those who are following.

Boldness doesn't mean rushing in without a plan. Boldness is a quiet confidence that you (and those around you) possess the knowledge, insight, skills, and resources to accomplish the task at hand.

> **"Boldness isn't something you are born with.**
> **You either choose it, or you don't."**
> **Mike Yaconetti**

Black Belt Leaders in Life equip others. The best leaders are people developers. You make the team better by pouring into the lives of those around you.   Another of King Solomon's quips of wisdom is the phrase, *"As iron sharpens iron, so one person sharpens another."*

When you take the time to equip and train those around you, you inspire them to pursue their own personal growth journey. That in turn, makes the whole team better. When you speak into the lives of those around you, encouraging them through your input, it is transformational. It tells those who are following you, "*I believe in you.*" That is truly inspirational.

Equipping and training others gives them insight, knowledge, and wisdom into things they may not know yet. By sharing your life experience, your knowledge and wisdom, with those who are following, you're helping them discover new and innovative ways of problem-solving, growing and maturing as a leader.

Pouring into the lives of your followers is preparing them for the day they will be asked to lead. Imagine you as a leader, leading a team of highly skilled individuals who can lead in their own right. What a powerhouse that creates. Now, you and your team can take on, and accomplish, even more. You now have equipped those around you to pursue their own black belt in leadership as they, in turn, equip and train others.

Results are multiplied, exponentially, as your team's capacity to lead others is expanded. This comes as a result of you continually equipping, pouring into, and adding value to those who are on the journey with you. This is where significance can happen. But you can't achieve significance as an individual, or as a team, if you haven't prepared yourself, and your team, for what lies ahead.

> *"We must open the doors of opportunity. But we must also equip our people to walk through these doors."*
> **Lyndon B. Johnson**

Black Belt Leaders in Life are loyal. Loyalty starts at home, first with yourself and then with your family. Loyalty and integrity are the lynchpins of success in life, for without them you will never accomplish anything significant, nor have a following or a cause that lives beyond your days on the earth.

If you can't be loyal to yourself, how can you demand loyalty from others? If you can't be a person of integrity, one who can be trusted even when no one is looking, then how can you demand and expect others to live lives of integrity? One of the greatest things that can be said of you as a leader, and as a person, is that you are known as a man or woman of integrity.

Leaders must also be loyal to their calling. Whatever your passion is, your dream that you are pursuing, you have to remain committed to that. Consistency is so very important, as it is the glue that keeps others connected to you in the pursuit of your dream or the task or goal of your organization. There are a lot of causes one can pursue, but remaining loyal to the one calling that inspires you, compels you, and that you are passionate about, is what is required to see that dream become reality.

Loyalty requires a singular focus on the task at hand. Integrity to your calling means you keep it at the forefront of all that you do, so your team buys into that passion and they too become singularly focused about seeing that come to pass. For an NFL football team, it's the Superbowl. For an NBA basketball team, it's the NBA Championship. What is it for you?

A leader who is loyal won't compromise. Like a soldier who has been given a command, you press on to accomplish the task at hand without wavering until the mission is accomplished. A leader is a man or woman of integrity that governs what they think, say and do. Integrity governs how you live your life

"Soldiers, when committed to a task, can't compromise. Its unrelenting devotion to the standards of duty and courage, absolute loyalty to others, not letting the task go until it's done."

John Keegan

To become a black belt in leadership, you understand that leadership is transformational. It changes who you are. It alters how you live life. How you think, what you say, what you do, and why you do it change. Simon Sinek's *Start With Why* speaks to the life change that takes place when you discover your why, and how this literally transforms the who, what, how, when, and where of your life.

You find fulfillment and purpose when you find your why, and it is transformative. For the leader, finding the why you lead not only changes you, it transforms those who are following as they see and hear you share with passion the WHY of your leadership. This is how inspirational leaders such as Mahatma Gandhi, Nelson Mandela, Jesus of Nazareth, the prophet Mohammed, Gautama Buddha, Mother Teresa, and Martin Luther King, Jr. have brought about transformational change in their followers and left their lasting, memorable mark in the world.

The power of personal transformation in a leader enlarges their dream. As you personally grow and mature as a leader, you will change and your leadership dream will enlarge. Your passion for this will expand, as will your influence. The more you change, the more you will tell your story, your vision for the future, with an inspirational tone that will call others to join you on the journey.

A leader transformed leaves a lasting legacy that lives beyond their years. Remember, Jesus started with a ragtag group of

12 disciples, that expanded to 120, then to 3000, and today over 2.2 billion people around the world profess Christianity. As of this writing, John Maxwell started teaching leadership in a small church about 25 years ago. Today, John Maxwell has over 20,000 trained speakers, trainers, and coaches in 160 countries. Together, they are carrying his transformational leadership message to the ends of the earth.

What about you? What will be your legacy as a leader? How will you be remembered? Will you (like Jesus, Mohammed, Buddha, Gandhi or Mandela) have those who will perpetuate your dream into the future? Or, will you be like the character described in this excerpt from the poem, *The Indispensable Man* written by Saxon White Kessinger?

"Take a bucket and fill it with water,
Put your hand in it up to the wrist,
Pull it out and the hole that's remaining
Is a measure of how you'll be missed."

How many worthwhile charities, organizations and causes have been started by men and women who were transformed, who saw a cause worth committing their life to? How many lives can you touch, influence and change today, and even years after you are gone, through transformational leadership?

To the martial arts practitioner, the test for 1st Degree black belt is a culmination of years of study and training, hard work, and a lot of sweat and tears. Don't forget my dad started the martial arts at the age of 70 and it was transformational to watch the change in his life as he worked his way through the ranks. Here was a man who initially told me, *"John, I'm too old for the martial arts."* He quickly became a man who showed up for class 3-4 times a week.

Here's what you don't know. My dad received third-degree burns over much of his lower body and torso as a 12-year old child and spent nearly a year in the hospital recovering. Doctors were unsure he would ever walk again, and even today, at the age of 82, his body bears the scars of burnt flesh, and skin grafts taken from other parts of his body. He suffers from Scoliosis, an unnatural curvature of the spine.

Exercises initially had to be modified; some remained that way because of his physical condition. He received no special treatment because he was my Dad. He was treated just like another student in the dojo. Like the rest of us, he went home hot, sweaty and tired after class. There were times he went home bloodied and bruised. Karate is a contact sport, and at times accidents can and do happen.

But he persevered through the pain, the discomfort, the physical challenges and the mental duress of learning and remembering a multitude of punches, kicks, blocks, and kata (stylized forms and patterns), as well as the practical self-defense applications of our martial arts system. I watched my dad pursue with passion something he was willing to sacrifice for, and it was my privilege to help him tie his 1st-degree black belt in Shorin Ryu Karate around his waist at the age of 75.

My dad transformed, as did those around him. He inspired many of our younger adults with his determination and good demeanor. Dad, always the encourager, added value to those around him. He took it upon himself to start helping those who were behind him in rank, so they could learn and progress. As he gave back to others, he demonstrated the true nature of a servant leader. He led by example, and his willingness to help those behind him on the journey learn from his experience so they could one day surpass him and do the same for others.

Being a transformational leader doesn't mean that you change the world. It may be a single life you influence, but that life may go on and change the world. Perhaps your leadership and influence help you positively impact the next Billy Graham, Bill Gates, Steve Jobs, Louis Pasteur, George Washington Carver, Mother Teresa, Winston Churchill or Thomas Edison.

If your transformational influence as a Black Belt Leader in Life does nothing more than mold and shape the lives of your spouse and your children, is that not a cause worth pursuing? If your influence helps to instill positive moral character traits in a young boy or girl who goes on to live an exemplary life as a role model for others, is that not a reason to pursue excellence in how you live your own life?

Being a Black Belt Leader in Life means you've internalized the positive character attributes of servant leadership, and you live them out in your daily routine. You add value to people. You are purposeful about seeing the good in others, encouraging and equipping them as a mentor and a role model. You intentionally do the small things daily that lead to long term success in life.

Once you've internalized these traits, and begin to live them out, you begin to do this spontaneously, as it becomes a part of who you are. You no longer have to stop and think, "*As a leader, what would I do?*" Through your daily routine, you LIVE OUT leadership so that it becomes WHO YOU ARE. That's "*Mushin*".

Leadership Mushin is transformational. It reshapes your thinking and your attitude, which in turn govern with your saying and doing. It changes who you are, what you do, and what you become. That, in turn, transforms those around you, and together you can literally change the world, one person at a time. You can summit your Mt. Everest, as you lead others to greatness.

Two of John Maxwell's more famous quotes speak to the importance, and the power of transformation: (1) *"Everything rises and falls on leadership."* (2) *"Leadership is influence, nothing more, nothing less."*

Being a Black Belt Leader in Life requires you to understand and embrace that EVERYTHING in your life, and the lives of those who are following you, rises and falls on YOUR leadership, or the lack thereof. The influence of a transformational servant leader is powerful, it is life-changing. It can truly change the world, one life at a time.

"Yes, your transformation will be hard. Yes, you will feel frightened, messed up and knocked down. Yes, you'll want to stop. Yes, it's the best work you'll ever do."
Robin Sharma

White Belt	Level One	**B**elieve
Yellow Belt	Level Two	**L**earn
Orange Belt	Level Three	**A**ccountability
Green Belt	Level Four	**C**ommunication
Blue Belt	Level Five	**K**inetic
Purple Belt	Level Six	**B**oldness
Brown Belt 1	Level Seven	**E**xcellence
Brown Belt 2	Level Eight	**L**oyalty
Brown Belt 3	Level Nine	**T**ransformation
Black Belt	Level Ten	**LEADERSHIP**

The Journey Continues...Now It Is Your Turn
Chapter Twelve

I took the reins of the United States Martial Arts Hall of Fame and International Martial Arts Council of America as the President and CEO in 2016. I never envisioned as a 13-year old teenager being enrolled in the martial arts to combat being bullied at school that I would have the privilege and honor of leading an organization that is dedicated to giving back to the martial arts community. I've met some amazing people, ranging from living legends who pioneered the martial arts growth in America to passionate men and women who work a full-time job and volunteer their time to teach a handful of students in a local YMCA, church or community center.

I've worked in the financial services industry for over three decades, serving both in the insurance and investment fields. I've authored books, articles, and blogs on finances, martial arts, and leadership, and have spoken to thousands of people in audiences in the United States, Central America, the Caribbean, and Africa. I've also served in various pastoral roles over the years, and have worked as a marketing and sales coach for more than two decades. I've been privileged to mentor and train individuals who have gone on to accomplish amazing, transformational things.

As I've reflected on all I've learned from this varied experience is that **anyone can lead**. It's a question of how well we lead that we each have to answer. We are all leading someone, somewhere. We all have influence over others around us. At the same time, we are also following someone, somewhere, and influenced by their input into our lives as well.

How well are you leading and influencing others?

I committed early on, by my Dad's example, to be a lifetime student of learning. At the age of 83, my dad is still reading books, watching podcasts online, and continuing to stretch himself. Nearly every time I see him, he tells me about an author whose book he's reading (or re-reading), a speaker he saw online or passing on an article or a newsletter.

Remember Ray Kroc's observation, *"When you're green, you're growing. When you're ripe, you start to rot."* Living the life of a leader is committing to a lifetime of learning. Leadership is a journey, not a destination. You can grow as a leader, but you never truly arrive.

Destination-disease, as it has been called, is the death knell for a leader. Once you believe that you have arrived, there is nothing more to learn, and you've gone as far as you can go, then your influence begins to fade. Remember Kodak? Once they "arrived" as the dominant force in the print film industry, they stopped being innovative, stopped growing, stopped leading, and their influence in the industry began to wane.

What got you to where you are today won't keep you where you find yourself tomorrow. You've got to be intentional about growing as a leader. You've got to keep stretching yourself, continually reaching for the next rung as you climb the leadership ladder. And you've got to be consistent because the secret to your success as a leader can be found in your daily routine.

So what does a personal growth plan actually look like?

It starts with that "man in the mirror" moment when you take an introspective look at yourself. You've got to know yourself before you can grow yourself, says John Maxwell. That requires you to take an honest inventory of you – your assets and liabilities.

- What are you passionate about? What motivates you?
- What are your strengths? Your weaknesses?
- What talents, skills do you possess that can be further developed?
- What opportunities are in front of you right now?
- What action steps do you need to take today to start on your leadership journey?
- What price are you willing to pay in order to grow?

No one takes the leadership journey alone. The greatest leaders are great because they understand they can (and do) learn from others who are further along the journey than they are. They choose to submit themselves to the teaching of others who can help them further develop their skills, talents, and abilities.

As a Black Belt Leader in Life, you are no different. You need to find someone who is ahead of you on their journey in an area that you need to grow in who is willing to speak into your life and submit yourself to their leadership. That can be through reading their books, listening to their podcasts, attending workshops where they are speaking, or enlisting them to be a personal coach or mentor. This is an investment you MUST make in yourself.

- In what areas do you need to grow?
- Who is gifted and successful that can help you in these areas?
- How will you gain access to their knowledge and influence?
- What price are you willing to pay in order to grow?

Remember, you can't grow in multiple areas at once. It is important that you identify one or two key areas you want to grow in, areas you are already strong in, and focus on these areas until you achieve some level of mastery. Then, and only then, can you consider adding to your growth journey in other areas of your life, while still growing in your strength zone.

Why focus on your strength zone? It's the area where you can see the greatest return on investment. In the business world, we learn about the Pareto Principle, also known as the 80/20 Rule. In sales, 80% of your production comes from the top 20% of your salespeople. So, if I help the top 20% get even better, I increase my opportunity to see a greater return through more sales.

The same principle applies as you evaluate your strengths, gifts, and talents. There are a LOT of things you can do, but out of all the things you CAN do, about 20% of those things you do exceptionally well. By focusing on growing in the areas you are already excelling at, you get EVEN BETTER at these skills, traits or abilities and your results reflect that.

- Make a list of all your strengths, skills and talents.
- Identify the Top 10 that you're best at
- Rank them in order from 1-10
- Work on growing in areas 1 and 2

For example, if you are ranked as an "A-player" in speaking and a "C-player" in organization, it's much easier to improve your ranking to an "A+" in speaking than to improve your ranking to an "A" in organization. Focusing on your strength zone allows you to hone those unique skills and talent that you've been given that will give you a better opportunity to achieve success as a leader in this area than working in your weakness zone.

Personal development tools like Real Life Management, DISC, Myers-Briggs or other analysis tools can help you understand how you're "hardwired," and can help you identify and quantify your strength zone when it comes to your unique skill set. Wayne Nance's *The 3 Minute Difference* was an awakening in my life as I discovered how I (and those around me) lived life and how my internal hardwiring impacted my relationships, my health, my finances, and my leadership style.

It's also important that you remain consistent, doing the small things daily that will lead you long term success as a Black Belt Leader in Life. That means keeping yourself in an environment that is conducive to learning and growing. I was recently on a call with John Maxwell where he reminded us that motivation may get us going, but it is through discipline and consistency that we keep going.

That means we stay the course, even when times are difficult. One of the books I've enjoyed sharing with young people is John Maxwell's *Sometimes You Win, Sometimes You Learn*. Even life's difficulties and challenges can teach us something if we are willing to learn. How many coaches take their teams through a video review of their last performance? They don't do that to celebrate the win all over again. They do this to look for areas where individuals, and the team, can improve.

That's where reflection comes in. Taking the time to put life on pause to see what lessons our mistakes, our shortcomings, and our failures may be trying to teach us. Albert Einstein has been credited in some circles with saying that insanity is doing the same thing over and over again and expecting a different result.

In the movie, *Edge of Tomorrow*, Tom Cruise plays a soldier forced into a suicide mission and is forced to relive the same bloody battle scene over again and again. Throughout the movie, you see him reflect on what went wrong the day before and what could be learned from this mistake. The next day, he traverses a little further, until he makes yet another mistake and dies, only to relive the same day again and again. Each time, he journeys a little further, continually learning from his prior mistakes, until he completes his mission. Even after the mission is completed, the journey doesn't end and life goes on.

Your leadership journey will be much the same way. There will be times you fall short, make a mistake, or miss the mark. Taking a pause in your journey to evaluate what happened, why, and what can be learned from the experience is invaluable to your personal growth and maturity. I love John Maxwell's saying, *"Experience isn't the best teacher. Evaluated experience is."*

Black Belt Leaders in Life are passionate about what they do, and the difference they can make in the world. They understand their WHY, and that in turn influences their WHO, WHAT, WHEN, WHERE and HOW. Simon Sinek's *Start With Why* is a must-read for the leader who wants to truly discover their WHY and, in turn, channel that into becoming a difference maker in the world.

Understanding your WHY is a catalyst for growth. When you know your WHY, you become passionate about wanting to grow, to learn, so you can see your WHY come to fruition. You realize there is no finish line in leadership, and that your WHY will push you outside your comfort zone and cause you to believe the impossible is truly achievable.

- What is your WHY?
- What is your impossible dream?
- Are you learning something new every day?

I want to challenge you to embrace leadership as a lifestyle. In our martial arts school, we taught values-based leadership to our students. It's a trend I'm hoping the entire global martial arts community will embrace. Think of the good we could do in the world of martial arts instructors, sports coaches, school teachers, pastors, business owners, and volunteer coordinators would begin to embody values-based leadership as a lifestyle and model it to those who are following.

To the martial arts community...

As a black belt instructor, you are in a unique position to have the opportunity to mentor and train young men and women, sometimes influencing their lives for several years. If you could put the same passion into modeling and teaching leadership that you do into teaching the technical aspects of the martial arts, think of the impact.

If these young lives leave your school with a black belt, confident they can defend themselves, that's an amazing achievement. If they can also leave your school knowing how to lead their own lives well, make good choices, add value to others and become an influencer for positive change in their community, what an even greater achievement that would be.

To business owners and entrepreneurs...

You're in business for a reason, to deliver an exceptional product or service to the public, and profit from those efforts. If you can also influence those in your employ to become leaders in their own right, to learn to add value to their Team Members and the public they serve, how much more efficient, and profitable, does your business become?

If you can help your employees identify and develop their unique strengths, and teach them to help others on the Team to do the same, how much better does your workplace become when everyone is helping to bring out the best in each other? Imagine harnessing the untapped potential in each Team member as together you release the creative power within. What could your Team dream, accomplish and achieve as each member learns to lead himself or herself and to lead together to make the impossible become reality.

To the church community...

According to a 2016 Barna Research study, one of the greatest deficits in the church today is a lack of leadership. This has led to the church losing influence in the local, national and international stage. By embracing and living out true servant leadership, and teaching these truths to their congregations, churches could empower individuals to learn to lead themselves and husbands and wives to lead their families.

The Great Commission is a call to leadership. *"Go, Teach, Make Disciples"* was the final set of instructions given to the followers of Jesus. Leadership is first about modeling, internalizing the values of leadership in your daily lives. Secondly, leadership is about equipping those who are following to also become leaders themselves. Thirdly, leadership is a discipleship process where we commit to a lifetime of learning and passing that learning on to others who are on the same journey.

To the education community...

Providing a world-class education is essential to helping the next generation see success in the real world. While English, Math, Science, Geography, History, Art and Music are important skill sets to learn, how much better would our students be equipped if we taught them, from an early age, the values and character traits of leadership?

If we taught students to add value to others, to commit to being lifetime learners, and to focus on being a positive change-agent in their local communities, what could be the long-term impact in their school, their homes, and their city? If students learned to value, and appreciate, the unique potential within each of their classmates, and worked together to develop that potential so that everyone could learn to lead themselves and others, we would raise up a generation of young adults that add value to others, live their lives intentionally, and together achieve great things.

To volunteer organizations...

You are passionate about what you do, as you are giving your time and resources for a cause you believe in. Many of you are helping those less fortunate than you by offering not just a handout, but a *"hand up"* in life. Helping those who are struggling to see their amazing potential within, and teaching them to develop the leader inside, can truly give them that important next step to turning their lives around and achieve success in life.

Helping others learn to see and respond to the lessons that life is trying to teach them and deal with the challenges of life empowers them to make better choices, improve their situation, and learn to grow through adversity. As they learn to lead themselves, they can share what they're learning with others who are also dealing with similar challenges, and together they can improve the lives of those less fortunate. Everyone wins.

So now, it's your turn. You've seen what it takes to become a Black Belt Leader in Life. The question I would like to leave you with is this: ***What are you going to do with what you've learned?***

I would like to challenge you to go back to the first of this book, starting with Chapter Two, and spend the next 30 days applying the key teachings from each chapter into your daily routine. Remember, the secret to your success is found in your daily routine, so we're focusing on growing and internalizing these character traits into your daily habits.

After you've focused on internalizing Belief, then move on to Chapter Three and spend 30 days internalizing the character trait of Learning, all while continuing the daily habit of believing. After 30 days of Learning, then spend the next 30 days focused on being Accountable, all while continuing the daily habit of believing and learning.

I think you get the picture. After 9 months, you will have internalized 9 important character traits of a Black Belt Leader in Life – making each of these values a part of your daily routine. As you do this, your leadership level will increase. As you learn to lead yourself better, you become a better leader of others.

You will discover as you do this your influence over those who are following you will also increase. The number of people who are following your lead will increase as well. As you take what you're teaching and model it before those you're leading, they too will grow. You will find increasing opportunities to pour into their lives as you look for ways to add value to others.

You will be living the life of a Black Belt Leader in Life, discipling those who are following you as you replicate yourself through those you are raising up to take your place and expand your influence over time. The lasting legacy you leave behind will be the leaders you have helped to raise up who will take what they have learned and instill these character values in the lives of the next generation of leaders under their tutelage.

Black Belt Leaders in Life are perpetual students of leadership, so let this be the start of your leadership journey. It is one of the most difficult, and most rewarding, journeys you will ever embark upon – and one of the few that is truly life-changing.

May you lead…and lead well, as a Black Belt Leader in Life.

Recommended Reading & Resources

Being a lifetime learner requires that you consistently invest time in your own growth and education. The most productive minds in the world set aside at least 30-60 minutes a day for reading. What type of content do they read? Books and articles devoted to education, inspiration, motivation, and leadership.

Let me challenge you to set a personal goal to read a minimum of ONE book a month, 12 books in a year. As you're reading, highlight or underline important thoughts or ideas, and take a few moments to journal or record these thoughts where you can readily access them in the future.

While not an exclusive list, this will definitely get you started on your personal growth journey. Some of these are classics, while others are more recent literary works.

Developing the Leader Within You 2.0
John Maxwell

Think and Grow Rich
Napoleon Hill

How to Win Friends & Influence People
Dale Carnegie

Sometimes You Win, Sometimes You Learn
John Maxwell
(Separate Versions Available for Kids, Teens, and Adults

Start With Why
Simon Sinek

The 3-Minute Difference
Wayne Nance

The 15 Invaluable Laws of Growth
John Maxwell

The Go-Giver & The Go-Giver Leader
Bob Berg

The 21 Irrefutable Laws of Leadership
John Maxwell

Triggers: Creating Behavior that Lasts
Marshall Goldsmith

The Fred Factor
Mark Sanborn

Everyone Communicates, Few Connect
John Maxwell

As a Man Thinketh
James Allen

You Don't Need a Title to be a Leader
Mark Sanborn

Becoming a Person of Influence
John Maxwell

The Fred Factor 2.0
Mark Sanborn

Put Your Dream to the Test
John Maxwell

About the Author

John Terry
"The Black Belt Leader"

A two-time martial arts Hall of Fame inductee, John brings years of experience to personal and corporate coaching, training and mentoring.

John brings a warm sense of humor and a quick wit that immediately connects with his audience as he delivers an insightful message that inspires and motivates while challenging those in attendance to grow and aspire to greatness.

Author and in-demand public speaker, John is an Executive Director with The John Maxwell Team and has been trained as a speaker, trainer, and coach with JMT. He has also been certified in Real Life Management and is a DISC Certified Consultant.

When you're looking for Black Belt quality results in leadership, communication, personal development or relationships, John delivers black belt excellence in coaching and training with wit and wisdom.

For More Information or Scheduling Details:

Black Belt Leadership
www.beablackbeltleader.com

Teach Your Children to Dream BIG!

Available on Amazon.com

Ebenezer's Journal
By: Jessie Terry

Join Ebenezer as he uses the POWER OF IMAGINATION to transform Dr. Lime's School of Normal Monsters into something amazing.

Inspire your child to "DREAM BIG" as Ebenezer awakens the dreams and potential of his fellow students to transform his school and his community.

A fun read that can start young children (ages 5-8) on their own personal growth journey. Help them discover and tap into the incredible, unlimited potential within. This entertaining book will inspire your children to live extraordinary lives s they learn to inspire others to pursue their own dreams and aspirations for the future. Buy your copy of Ebenezer's Journal today. Only $9.95 on Amazon.com

ABOUT THE AUTHOR: Jessie Terry, is a speaker, trainer, and coach with The John Maxwell Team. She is passionate about inspiring children to pursue their dreams and see the unlimited potential within them to be influencers and world-changers. At the age of 17, Jessie traveled to Guatemala to work with underprivileged youth. A year later, she traveled to Cameroon, Africa to work with autistic and special needs children. Jessie has spoken at the International Maxwell Conference, the United States Martial Arts Hall of Fame and other venues across the United States, inspiring a new generation of young people to make a difference.

Ebenezer's Journal is Jessie's first children's book. She hopes to challenge and inspire children to be extraordinary in the way they live their lives, to pursue BIG dreams and to make a positive difference by adding value to others.

Faith-Based Martial Arts

Christian Martial Arts

The Passion. The Calling. The Journey.

How to Effectively Incorporate Faith-Based
Principles Into Your Martial Arts Practice

John L. Terry, III

This book is a "How To" guide both for the instructor who is a believer interested in incorporating faith-based principles into a martial arts program, and for the instructor who is already sharing Christ in his or her school.

This book presents proven principles, concepts, and methodology from a number of sources that can be adapted or molded to fit any given martial arts system or style. It is intended to be a resource to inspire us all to "Go, Teach, and Make Disciples."

Written by a martial arts instructor who successfully built a multi-location retail martial arts business that was openly faith-based. John has also helped a number of school owners either start a faith-based program on their own or served as a mentor and a resource to those who are already teaching martial arts from a faith-based perspective.

Available on Amazon.com for only $13.99

The Christian Martial Arts Council is a martial arts association for faith-based schools, instructors and students. It is also a place for Christian martial artists who may not be teaching or training from a faith-based perspective, but want to fellowship with like-minded martial artists.

CMAC is a sister association to the International Martial Arts Council of America, one of the premier martial arts associations in the world. IMAC is the sponsoring organization for the United States Martial Arts Hall of Fame.

IMAC and CMAC host a National Training Camp annually. This 3-day event features world-class martial arts instruction, with a different style or system taught in each session. It is an opportunity to celebrate the diversity of the global martial arts community, share training tips, and interact with school owners and instructors.

www.imacusa.com

www.ChristianMartialArtsCouncil.com

Black Belt Leadership 101

What it Takes to Be a Black Belt Leader in Life

Discussion Guide

Black Belt Leadership 101
Making It Real

This discussion guide is intended to provide you with an outline to help you apply what you've learned from each chapter in this book. It can also be used as a discussion guide if you're using this content as part of a small group or mastermind discussion.

It is not enough just to passively read this book and check it off as "done". If you're not taking the time to reflect on what you have already experienced and how it applies to your personal growth journey, you're not getting the full benefit of this leadership teaching.

If you're a martial arts school owner, you can use this discussion guide (or use the companion Martial Arts Discussion Guide) to lead a *"Mat Chat"* with your students, or as content for your Black Belt or Leadership Club in your school. Remember, real leaders equip others to lead, and do so by modeling Black Belt Leadership before them. John Maxwell says, *"People do what people see."*

Keeping a Leadership Journal to write down your thoughts and observations as you're reading this book will help you capture ideas, quips and quotes you can refer back to in the future. You can also document the source of the information, and reference the applicable page numbers, making it easier to go back to the source material in the future.

To take this a step farther, find an accountability partner who will either go through this book with you or at least will hold you responsible to the process of going through this material yourself. This is where a small group setting (also known as a mastermind) becomes so powerful, as you become mutually responsible to each other, as you learn and grow to become Black Belt Leaders in Life together.

If you're meeting as a small group to work through this leadership journey together, it is important that you establish on the front end the right of each member to speak into the lives of other members of the group without recourse.

When iron sharpens iron, it is uncomfortable. But when people are men and women of integrity, working together to not only improve themselves but the lives of those around them, honest communication is invaluable to each member's personal growth as a leader.

Lastly, as you're working through each of these essential character traits of a Black Belt Leader in Life, visual reminders can be invaluable. One tip I teach is to use a Post-It® note to write down the trait you are working on and stick it on your bathroom mirror. As an alternative, you can use a Dry Erase marker and actually write this on the mirror.

Then, every morning when you're preparing for your day, you have to have that "Man in the Mirror" moment when you are reminded of your task to embody a specific leadership trait into your daily routine. And when you come home at the end of your day, you get to have that second "Man in the Mirror" moment when you have to look yourself squarely in the eye and grade yourself on how well (or not so well) you did in living out that leadership trait in your daily routine that day.

And...the next morning, you get to do it all over again. So, let's get started making Black Belt Leadership real in your life...

Chapter One
Lead Like a Black Belt

Leadership: (1) the action of leading a group of people or an organization; (2) the state or position of being a leader; (3) the leaders of an organization, country, etc.

Take an inventory of your talent, abilities and skill set, and ask others who are close to you to do their own inventory of your talent, abilities and skill set. Compare these lists and look for areas where there is alignment.

Take a personal assessment to help you evaluate your unique strengths and weaknesses. Among these are Real Life Management and DISC.

1. How do you personally define leadership?

Write a one-paragraph definition of leadership, as if you were writing a hiring advertisement. If you were going to hire a leader, what would be the skills, abilities, experience, training, and resources you would want a leader to have if you were going to hire this individual.

2. What does leadership look like to you on a day-to-day basis? What are the things you believe a leader should say, do, and model before others who are following?

Take your hiring advertisement and flesh this out to define the activities you would expect a leader to do daily, weekly, monthly, etc. What metrics would you use to measure this leader's success?

3. Do you see yourself as leadership material? Why would people want to follow your leadership?

4. If you could only lead in one specific area, what would that be?

Write a brief description of how you would lead in this particular area of your strength, and what the benefit to others would be as a result of your leading in this specific area.

5. Where do leadership deficits exist in society today? What is the impact on society because of these deficits?

6. If you were to give an honest evaluation of where you are as a student of leadership today, what color belt would you be wearing? Why?

Black Belt Leadership – Ranking System

White Belt	Level One	**B**elieve
Yellow Belt	Level Two	**L**earn
Orange Belt	Level Three	**A**ccountability
Green Belt	Level Four	**C**ommunication
Blue Belt	Level Five	**K**inetic
Purple Belt	Level Six	**B**oldness
Brown Belt 1	Level Seven	**E**xcellence
Brown Belt 2	Level Eight	**L**oyalty
Brown Belt 3	Level Nine	**T**ransformation
Black Belt	Level Ten	**LEADERSHIP**

Chapter Two
The Power of Believing.

Belief: (1) an acceptance that a statement is true or that something exists; (2) trust, faith, or confidence in someone or something.

SUMMARY – Level One (White Belt)

"Nothing can be achieved that you do not believe."
John Terry

1. Believe in the value of leadership.
2. Believe in the need for leadership.
3. Believe in your calling as a leader.
4. Believe you can grow and mature as a leader.

1. King Solomon said, *"As a man thinketh, so his he."* What was the point Solomon was trying to get across by this statement? Why is believing a necessary character trait for a leader? Explain.

2. Phillip of Macedonia, Alexander the Great's father said, *"An army of deer led by a lion is more to be feared than an army of lions led by a deer."* Mark Sanborn, author of You Don't Need a Title to be a Leader, added, *"An army of lions led by a lion is to e feared most of all, for it is unstoppable."*

Write down your thoughts on these two statements as they pertain to believing and acting as a leader.

3. Who do you know that believes in something so much they would be willing to do anything for this cause? What about this person's belief personally inspires or motivates you?

4. President John F. Kennedy inspired a nation when he proclaimed that by the end of the 1960s, we would put a man on the moon. He believed this was possible, and that the ingenuity of the scientists at NASA could make this come to pass. Kennedy shared his belief, and a few short years later Neil Armstrong took mankind's first steps on the moon.

Why is it important to share what you believe as a leader with those you are leading? What is the benefit of doing this?

5. It is said that 10,000 hours of practice is required to become an expert in any given field. Based on the amount of time you're devoting to growing in a particular area of strength, how long will it take you to become an expert in this field? Is this doable?

6. What is your personal belief on the importance of growing as a leader? What action steps are you currently taking today? What additional action steps are you willing to commit to in order to grow?

Create a growth calendar, with specific times set aside daily for reading, listening to podcasts, watching leadership videos. Track your progress and give yourself a grade (A through F) at the end of 30 days.

Chapter Three
The Necessity of Learning

Learn: (1) to gain or acquire knowledge or skill in (something) by study, experience or being taught; (2) to commit to memory; (3) to become aware of (something) by information or from observation.

SUMMARY – Level Two (Yellow Belt)

"A lifetime of learning equips for a lifetime of leading."
John Terry

1. Commit to a lifestyle of learning.
2. Leaders must grow to become effective.
3. Learning requires humility and openness.
4. Leaders must be followers.

1. Mahatma Gandhi said, *"Life as if you were to die tomorrow. Learn as if you were to live forever."* What was the point Gandhi was trying to make to his followers?

2. Why is it so important we commit to a lifetime of learning? Explain.

Name someone from recent history who demonstrates a lifetime learning attitude. What parallels can you draw that will help you on your own personal growth journey?

3. Humility is defined as having a modest or low view of one's own importance. Why is being humble such an essential character trait to effective learning? Why is it difficult for arrogant or close-minded (opinionated) people to learn and grow?

4. Who are the people you are following? What does their input into your life look like?

Take a moment to make a list of the people who are serving as leaders or teachers in your life. In what areas of your life are they adding value? Are there additional things you could be learning from these individuals that could help you grow and mature as a leader?

5. Leadership is others-centered. How do leaders demonstrate this to those who are following?

Make a list of some of the ways leaders can effectively add value to those who are following, and discuss briefly the benefit that comes as a result of serving others.

6. Remember, it is easier to improve upon your strengths than your weaknesses. While you can improve both, your greater return on investment comes from honing the things you do well, so they are done even better. And while you may be good at several things, you're only great at one or two that you do better than everything else.

Identify one or two specific areas related to leadership you would like to grow in. What is your plan to grow in these areas?

Chapter Four
The Importance of Accountability

Accountable: (1) (of a person, organization, or institution) required or expected to justify actions or decisions; responsible; (2) explicable or understandable.

SUMMARY – Level Three (Orange Belt)

"Neither age nor experience matters when it comes to being personally responsible for any and all of my outcomes."
Kory Livingstone

1. You must be accountable to yourself.
2. You must be accountable to your mentors.
3. You must be accountable to the process.
4. You must be accountable to your followers.

1. Accountability is being responsible to others. By definition responsible means: (1) having an obligation to do something, or having control over or care for someone, as part of one's job or role; (2) being the primary cause of something and so able to be blamed or credited for it; (3) (of a job or position) involving important duties, independent decision-making, or control over others; (4) having to report to (a superior or someone in authority) and be answerable to them for one's actions; (5) capable of being trusted; (6) morally accountable for one's behavior.

Why should a leader be accountable? Who should he or she be accountable to as a leader?

2. Identify two leaders from recent history, one who has taken personal responsibility for his or her actions, and another who has not. What can be learned from their story?

3. In *The 21 Irrefutable Laws of Leadership* John Maxwell explains the Law of the Inner Circle. John says, "*A leader's potential is determined by those closest to him.*" As much as 95% of a person's future occurs as the result of the influence of the top 5 in your inner circle.

What does this statement say to you as it pertains to accountability? Make a list of the people who are closest to you, your inner circle of influencers, and identify your Top 5. If 95% of your future is the result of your Top 5, what does your future look like?

4. One of my favorite quotes from John Maxwell is, "*If you think you're leading, and no one is following, then you're only taking a walk.*" Thinking about this statement in the light of accountability, what are some reasons people may find themselves thinking they are leading, but in reality, no one is following their lead?

5. Being accountable to yourself, to your followers and to your teachers makes sense to most people. Being accountable to the process is something many leaders haven't given much thought to.

What does it mean to be accountable to the process?

6. King Solomon wrote, "*As iron sharpens iron, so are the wounds of a friend.*" How are the thoughts and insights of an ancient King relevant in today's world of leadership and accountability?

Chapter Five
The Art of Communication

Communication: (1) the imparting or exchanging of information or news; (2) a letter or message containing information or news; (3) the successful conveying or sharing of ideas and feelings; (4) social contact; (5) means of connection between people or places, in particular; (6) the means of sending or receiving information, such as telephone lines or computers.

SUMMARY – Level Four (Green Belt)

"Wise men speak because they have something to say. Fools because they have to say something."

Plato

1. Communication matters.
2. What you communicate matters.
3. How you communicate matters.
4. Clarity and consistency matters in communication.

1. Humans are unique in the animal kingdom when it comes to means of communication. We are social creatures, and the ability to communicate thoughts and ideas are key to social interaction.

What are some of the ways we communicate thoughts and ideas today? What are the various communication channels we have available to help us convey a message?

2. Miscommunication between two or more people is perhaps one of the most common shortcomings of mankind

today. Make a list of the ways people can miscommunicate with others.

What are some of the ways we can improve on communication?

3. Another of King Solomon's wise sayings is, *"The power of life and death are in the tongue."* Explain how this statement is relevant when it comes to being an effective leader and communicator today.

4. According to research by Dr. Albert Mehrabian, 7% of a message is conveyed with words, 38% through vocal elements (such as inflection) and 55% through nonverbal elements (such as facial expressions, gestures, and posture).

If as much as 93% of our communication is more than mere words, how much thought do you give to your non-verbal "saying"? What steps to you need to take to make sure your verbal and non-verbal communication are saying the same thing?

5. Why are clarity and consistency so important when you are communicating with others?

6. Studies reveal a well-told story not only stimulates the conscious (the intellect) but the subconscious (the emotions). Why is this important and why is story-telling one of the most effective ways to share thoughts or ideas with others?

Chapter Six
Leadership is Kinetic

Kinetic: relating to or resulting from motion.

SUMMARY – Level Five (Blue Belt)

*"Do you want to know who you are? Don't ask, ACT!
Action will delineate and define you."*

Thomas Jefferson

1. Leaders MUST lead. They must take decisive action.
2. Leaders must live out what they believe.
3. A leader's action must be duplicatable.
4. A leader's action must be consistent with his or her values and convictions.

1. Potential energy is stored energy, not yet released. Kinetic energy is energy in motion. How do leaders store potential energy, and how do they release it?

What do we mean by the statement leaders who are not leading are not leaders?

2. Thomas Jefferson said our actions delineate and define us. Your actions speak as loudly, and sometimes more loudly than your words. Remember John Maxwell's statement, *"People do what people see."*

Why is it so critical that leaders live out what they believe? What happens to their leadership if they don't?

3. If others cannot do what you do, you will act alone. One of the responsibilities of a leader is to lead in such a way that others can follow, and see success as well. If those who are following can't do what you do (or contribute in some meaningful way) they will eventually cease following.

What are some action steps you can take as a leader to help others "see and do" more effectively? How do you help those who are following you see success as well?

4. Integrity is defined as congruency (sameness) between your words and your deeds. It is considered the hallmark character trait of a Black Belt Leader in Life.

Why is personal integrity, living by your beliefs and convictions, so important for a leader?

5. Identify a leader who personifies kinetic leadership to you. What is it about their story that inspires or encourages you to be a kinetic leader yourself? What can you learn from their example?

6. Make a list of the ways you are leading today. How can you be more kinetic to improve in these areas? Write down 3 to 5 action steps you can take to be an action-focused leader.

Chapter Seven
Leaders Exhibit Boldness

Boldness: (1) not hesitating or fearful in the face of actual or possible danger or rebuff; (2) courageous and daring; beyond the usual limits of conventional thought or action.

SUMMARY – Level Six (Purple Belt)

**"Boldness isn't something you are born with.
You either choose it, or you don't."**
Mike Yaconetti

1. Boldness transforms you from "I Can't" to "I Can".
2. Boldness can be developed in the lives of others.
3. Boldness compounds results.
4. Boldness is not brashness.

1. A leader must be bold in word and deed. John Maxwell says that leaders should not only know more, they should go before others. That requires boldness.

What are some ways you are currently exhibiting boldness in your daily life as a leader?

2. Limiting thinking holds people back from achieving greatness. Boldness transforms you (and those who you're leading) from an "I Can't" mindset to a mindset that says, "I Can".

Identify a leader who lives out an "I Can" mindset in the way he or she lives life. What can you learn from their example?

3. Boldness has been defined as quiet confidence in your ability, an unwavering belief in yourself. is not something you're born with. It is something you learn, says Mike Yaconetti. You either choose to be bold, or you don't.

As a leader, how do you instill this quiet confidence and unwavering belief in oneself to those who you are leading?

4. Boldness is contagious. Far too many people live below their potential because they don't have a role model pouring into their lives, inspire them to pursue excellence as they discover and develop their strength zones.

As a leader, what are you doing to model boldness before others who are watching you lead? What action steps can you take, starting today, to be more intentional about leading with boldness?

5. NASA has been a model of boldness since the 1960s. The Apollo missions to the moon, the Hubble Space Telescope, the Space Shuttle, the International Space Station, Voyager spacecraft missions to other worlds, and now plans are underway to put boots on the surface of Mars.

What can we learn from NASA about boldness?

6. There is a fine line between boldly leading and leading with brashness (arrogance). What steps are you taking as a leader to assure that your boldness doesn't become arrogance?

Chapter Eight
The Essentialness of Equipping

Equip: (1) to supply with the necessary items for a particular purpose; (2) prepare (someone) mentally for a particular situation or task.

SUMMARY – Level Seven (Level 1 Brown Belt)

"We must open the doors of opportunity. But we must also equip our people to walk through these doors."
Lyndon B. Johnson

1. Equipping inspires
2. Equipping informs
3. Equipping prepares
4. Equipping multiples exponentially

1. It has been said that wisdom is the right use of knowledge. Knowledge not shared can never be rightly applied.   As a leader, you have a responsibility to pass on not only what you've learned, but how to apply it in real life.

What are some of the ways a leader can equip others?

2. Few things inspire success more than equipping. A follower who is equipped can take what he or she has learned and put it to good use. Success is within their grasp.

As a result of your leadership, what are your followers learning to do well?   Are there things you're not yet teaching them they should be learning to see even greater results?

3. One of the most important things a leader can do for those who are following is to prepare them for the task at hand. No team can be successful, or expect to win, that is not prepared. Having a game plan is good, but if the team isn't equipped and prepared to execute the plan, what good is it?

How should a leader prepare those who are following so they are equipped as a Team to win and see success?

4. The equipping process informs. It teaches what to do, when to do it, who to do it for (and with), where to do it, and why.

What is it you do as a leader?
When do you lead as a leader?
Who do you lead as a leader?
Where do you lead as a leader?
Why do you lead as a leader?

5. Leaders know that equipping one to influence another compounds the opportunity. Today, 2.2 Billion people follow the teachings of Jesus and 1.7 Billion people follow the teachings of Mohammed, two inspirational leaders whose life and legacy continue to spread through the world today.

Who are you equipping as a leader? Are you doing everything you can for them to prepare them to take your place?

6. What action steps are you taking as a leader to assure you are being effective in your equipping? How can you help those around you be better equipped to see success in their lives?

Chapter Nine
The Lasting Impact of Loyalty

Loyalty: (1) the quality of being loyal (giving or showing firm and constant support or allegiance to a person or institution) to someone or something; (2) a strong feeling of support or allegiance.

SUMMARY – Level Eight (Level 2 Brown Belt)

"Soldiers, when committed to a task, can't compromise. Its unrelenting devotion to the standards of duty and courage, absolute loyalty to others, not letting the task go until it's done."

John Keegan

1. Loyalty to yourself.
2. Loyalty to your family.
3. Loyalty to your calling.
4. Loyalty to your Team.

1. Loyalty has its roots in the character trait of integrity. Integrity is defined as the quality of being honest and having strong moral principles; moral uprightness; the state of being whole and undivided.

Write a brief description of loyalty's role in being a Black Belt Leader in Life.

2. In what ways do you see yourself as being loyal? Are there areas you can (and should) improve upon when it comes to being a person of loyalty and integrity?

3. My mom constantly admonished me to *"Be true to myself."* The story is told of Gandhi deferring to ask a young boy to stop eating sweets until he stopped eating sweets himself. Loyalty is being true to you.

Who do you know that is loyal or trustworthy? What do you admire about this person, and why?

4. Loyalty to family includes not just your blood relatives; it can also include team members on a sports team, fellow workers in a business endeavor, members of a church family, or your civic or community family.

Why is loyalty to your family so essential to your leadership?

5. Your calling is what defines you as a leader. It sets you apart and distinguishes you from everyone else. Your calling is what you were put on this earth to do. Great leaders live their lives pursuing their calling.

What is your calling as a leader? What is that ONE THING that you're passionate about?

6. If you're a leader, you have followers. You must be loyal to them, as they have embraced your calling and called it their own. Nothing of significance can be achieved by a Team who is not loyal to one another.

How do you maintain the trust of those who are following you?

Chapter Ten
The Power of Transformation

Transformation: (1) a thorough or dramatic change in form or appearance; (2) a process by which one figure, expression, or function is converted into another that is equivalent in some important respect but is differently expressed or represented.

SUMMARY – Level Nine (Level 3 Brown Belt)

"Yes, your transformation will be hard. Yes, you will feel frightened, messed up and knocked down. Yes, you'll want to stop. Yes, it's the best work you'll ever do."

Robin Sharma

1. Transformation changes you.
2. Transformation changes those around you.
3. Transformation enlarges your dream.
4. Transformation creates a legacy.

1. Transformation is a metamorphosis or marked change that takes place in the life of a person who has gone through a process that has refined or alerted them in some way. Transformation is change, and it begins within.

Looking back, what are some of the ways you have already experienced transformation in your personal life? Make a list of these, and add to this list as you experience further transformation along your growth journey in life.

2. Transformation on the inside is manifested on the outside. What we experience internally refines how we live our lives externally. How has your life changed as a result of your personal growth journey as a leader?

3. As you grow and mature as a leader, you should see this transformation spill over into the lives of those you are leading. Transformation is a catalyst that not only changes you, it changes those around you.

What changes do you see in the lives of those you are leading as a result of transformation taking place with you?   What additional changes do you want to see, and how are you working to transform yourself so this can also transform your followers?

4. As you grow and mature as a leader, your vision for the future expands. As you stretch to reach your potential, you soon discover that you're capable of much more than you dreamed. Your dreams enlarge as you realize the impossible can become reality.

How have your dreams grown as a leader since you started on your personal growth journey?   What is it that you're now reaching for that you hadn't even considered as a possibility before you began growing as a leader?

5. If, as a leader, you could be remembered for one thing when you're gone, what would you want that legacy to be? What steps are you taking to see that happen?   What additional steps are necessary?

6.   As a transformational leader, you should be asking yourself:

> How far can we go?
> How many lives can we change?
> What lasting impact can we make?
> What's next as we continue to move ahead?

Made in USA - North Chelmsford, MA
1103355_9781728966595
05.11.2020 1639